choose
to be
happily
married

choose
to be
happily
married

How Everyday Decisions Can Lead to *Lasting Love*

BONNIE JACOBSON, PhD
with ALEXIA PAUL

Avon, Massachusetts

This book is dedicated to Dr. Shera Aranoff Tuchman
and our woman's study group. For twenty years you
emphasized the idea that we are our choices.
Here is the product of all of that learning.

Published by
Adams Media, a division of F+W Media, Inc.
57 Littlefield Street, Avon, MA 02322. U.S.A.
www.adamsmedia.com

ISBN 10: 1-60550-625-7
ISBN 13: 978-1-60550-625-8
eISBN 10: 1-4405-0704-X
eISBN 13: 978-1-4405-0704-5

Printed in the United States of America.

10 9 8 7 6 5 4 3 2

Library of Congress Cataloging-in-Publication Data
is available from the publisher.

Although all of the stories in this book are derived from real life, no name or
specific is a complete replication of an original situation.

This publication is designed to provide accurate and authoritative information
with regard to the subject matter covered. It is sold with the understanding that
the publisher is not engaged in rendering legal, accounting, or other professional
advice. If legal advice or other expert assistance is required, the services of a competent professional person should be sought.
—From a *Declaration of Principles* jointly adopted by a Committee of the American Bar Association and a Committee of Publishers and Associations

Many of the designations used by manufacturers and sellers to distinguish their
product are claimed as trademarks. Where those designations appear in this book
and Adams Media was aware of a trademark claim, the designations have been
printed with initial capital letters.

This book is available at quantity discounts for bulk purchases.
For information, please call 1-800-289-0963.

CONTENTS

PART II: COMMUNICATION

ACKNOWLEDGMENTS

First and foremost, I am grateful to those who entrusted me with their relationships. A work of nonfiction of this scope would not be possible if wonderful people from all walks of life had not shared with me their private thoughts and feelings.

The next two most important midwives of this project are Stephanie Abou and Alexia Paul. I consider our group a dream team. Stephanie was determined to find just the right publisher and just the right editor, Chelsea King, to birth this book, and she did. I am grateful to everyone at Adams Media for providing a platform where I could concretize all that I have learned during the past forty years as a clinical psychologist.

Alexia and I have worked like a perfect hand-to-glove fit. She was always creative, conscientious, and supportive. Although I have never met her husband, Chris Walldorf, he was also a partner in making our enterprise ring with validity, as their relationship became the guinea pig upon which Alexia tested many of my theories.

My close friends and relatives, many of whom are in the same field as I am, have been extremely important in serving as sounding boards on the Turning Points, as well as the title. Some of these people are mentioned in conjunction with their own books within the body of *Choose to Be Happily Married*.

My students at New York University Applied Psychology Department have had important input, especially Emily Jacobs and Rachel Potek, who helped to develop the Emotional Turning Point Test.

I also appreciate the large group of people who were adventurous enough to take the Emotional Turning Point Test so that we could codify the data and create a scoring system.

Finally, a most personal gesture of gratitude to my husband, Arie Shapira. He has been my muse for practicing much of what I have discovered about the Turning Points. I also thank him for believing in me for the ten years it took to create this book from a dream to a reality. Without his participation, I would not have been able to experience the blessings and the challenges of lasting love.

PREFACE

"I am not what happened to me, I am what
I choose to become."

— Carl Jung

So many of the couples I have worked with over the past four decades have come to me feeling helpless at the demise of their marriages or long-term partnerships. "How did we get from there to here?" they ask. My response: The path from bliss to discontent is paved with everyday decisions that either build up or tear down your most intimate relationships.

I wrote *Choose to Be Happily Married* to give you an opportunity to recognize how the choices you make determine the outcome of an interpersonal event. I call these choices Turning Points—twenty-five either/or decisions, one or more of which are always present in a moment of stress with a loved one. Discovered through statistical analysis conducted by myself and my doctoral students, Dr. Emily Jacobs and Rachel Potek, these twenty-five choices are presented as chapters grouped into three categories—Flexibility, Communication, and Personal Power.

Choose to Be Happily Married demonstrates how to select a path that actually reflects your noblest choices, your best self. A beautiful Tibetan saying is, "Seeking happiness outside ourselves is like waiting for sunshine in a cave facing north." This book defines what you may *choose* to do if you hope to find happiness and survival in a love relationship.

Now for full disclosure: Sometimes I have not made the noble choice. But deciphering what constitutes a poor choice strengthens my potential for successful future decisions. And once you also understand the natural laws of sustaining love, you can take control of your actions instead of flailing about, helpless in the face of your basest emotions or leftover childhood trauma. With each choice, you can thoughtfully clear the way for a lifetime of love.

INTRODUCTION

"If you want to be loved, be lovable."

—Ovid

Finding lifelong happiness in a romantic relationship can be one of the great wonders—and challenges—of adult life. As easily as a loved one can be a port in the storm, a partner with whom to face the world, that person, by virtue of such proximity, can also be a source of angst. Love is not science. There are too many unknowns in the human heart to allow us to state a formula. How brave we are, that despite full knowledge of these mysteries, we sail ahead seeking happiness on a boat made of paper.

Is it possible to find enduring satisfaction within a bond that can sometimes seem fragile? Is there a way to avoid the pitfalls that so often send couples tumbling from love to disdain? I propose that the key to achieving contentment in our romantic lives—and, for that matter, in our lives as a whole—can be found in *how* we respond to unexpected disappointments and the inevitable upsets as well as the good times.

Staying in love after the initial flush of romance has faded is what they don't show us at the movies. The couple kisses as the sun sets, the credits roll, and that's that. But in reality, two people moving forward together are constantly changing, riding an ebb and flow of connection and disconnection. While some parts of any relationship may be wonderful, no love is perfect. This is a truth that disappoints many.

It is all too easy to focus on the imperfections within a relationship and submit to feeling powerless. He drinks to excess, she spends a lot or talks a great deal, he doesn't want to have as much sex as she does, her children are difficult, he has lost his job, and on and on.

These common human disappointments, however daunting they may seem, can serve as our classroom. And, often, the lesson is counterintuitive: In seeking to change someone else, it is actually only our own behavior that we can alter. In fact, these are the changes that can actually influence the couple environment.

Everyone's life is filled with situations in which our desires are thwarted, starting from day one when we want the sole attention and love from our caretaker. We soon learn that yearning for exclusive possession is unattainable and finally unacceptable. We then transfer this basic hunger onto others, onto objects, achievements, money, food, sex, and so on. All of these reconfigured desires are substitutes for the thing we cannot have, which is to own the first person with whom we fell in love—the person who sustained us from the very beginning. We subsequently proceed throughout life feeling a low-grade pulse of dissatisfaction.

In the best-case scenario, this yearning for an unmet feeling of satiation leads to a life worth living, one in which we pursue creativity and personal growth in an attempt to fulfill what is ultimately out of our reach: the early desire for complete possession of the one we love. Those who choose this path discover how to turn frustration into curiosity. The result can be a life filled with wonderment, inquisitiveness, and joy of living—not every day, and of course interspersed with despair, disappointment, and down days—but on the whole worth the effort.

However, the more common human emotion in my office, my life, and my friendships is people blaming their discontent on their partner's inadequacies. And as long as people are people, with their foibles, quirks, and—more ominously—dishonesty and addictions, placing blame will always be a tempting siren. What is more momentarily gratifying for some than yelling, screaming, and venting anger at a partner? Or for others, punishing a loved one's extreme spending habits, for example, by maintaining prolonged silences? This accusatory mentality does little permanent good. While we sit alone, nurturing our pet resentments, the possibility of lasting happiness remains elusive; things begin to fall apart.

How then do we consciously pursue and achieve such emotional awareness? Each moment of stress with our loved ones offers us an opportunity to make a choice: the decision to impulsively react or to respond with thoughtful intent.

EVERYDAY CHOICES

Imagine you are waiting outside a crowded theater and it's 8:05. He's late; it's raining; you just know the usher won't let you in once the curtain's up. You see your husband running toward you from the subway entrance, and in the next twenty seconds you must make a choice: you can greet him coldly (sure that he will register this as a continuation of an ongoing argument about how he never manages to leave work on time), thus committing yourselves to a tense evening. Or, you can take a deep breath and actively choose to give him the benefit of the doubt rather than making an instantaneous assumption of guilt. Did he spend too long chatting with a colleague on the way out the door? Maybe. Or, were the trains delayed? What if he lost five minutes helping an elderly man with his umbrella? Who knows? Ultimately, will you remember in ten years the reason he was five minutes late, or will the impression of an enjoyable evening at the theater endure?

Such an interaction may seem mundane, given how many similar scenes are played out each day, but by choosing the latter scenario you can actually make an informed decision, one that puts you on a path toward long-term joy over the short-term release of discomfort. This book explains the twenty-five most common choices—or Turning Points—that we make when we meet an unexpected or stressful moment in our lives. Many of these decisions happen under the radar and are the product of gut reactions and behaviors left over from habitual responses to stress developed in childhood. But by learning to recognize, for example, the subtle distinctions between good selfish and bad selfish, detaching rather than withdrawing, or cultivating patience over passivity, you can make each stressful encounter a constructive stepping stone in your relationship.

The distinguishing factor within each Turning Point is a decision to erect either a boundary or a barrier between yourself and a loved one. Boundaries allow a comfortable space to be maintained between two individuals. As in a dance, it is this space that helps a couple stay balanced and synchronized. An enjoyable, sustainable connection can be found as each respects the other's limits and limitations.

Barriers, on the other hand, scream "Don't touch me!" and "Get out!" When you are faced with a difficult interaction, barriers go hand-in-hand with reactive behavior. They are often the result of childhood unhappiness being played out in our adult lives. The result is a life lived according to established and familiar patterns dating from your earliest days that ultimately lead to isolation, loneliness, and finally, despair.

In the larger sense, within each Turning Point, the reactive choice creates a feeling of impermanence, the transience of being, and the capricious manner in which our lives hang on a whim. The responsive choice fosters a feeling of lastingness, open-ended goodwill to ourselves and those around us, gratitude, and a general feeling of well-being, or trust, in the face of whatever occurs.

This second alternative is the definition of everyday joy and the pathway that leads to longevity in a partnership. It is the path to lasting love. Joy is ultimately derived from how we respond both to unforeseen external events and to the emergence of unpredicted habits and customs in the partners we seemingly knew very well. Emotional control is a result of embracing our adult consciousness, our hard-won wisdom. And it has the extraordinary power to keep a love alive long after the credits roll.

HOW THIS BOOK WORKS

Choose to Be Happily Married can help relationships of all sorts, regardless of age or stage of togetherness, whether actually married or in a long-term committed union.

Before you begin, consider two ways to use this book:

1. If you wish to determine the specific problem area in your relationship, first take the Emotional Turning Point Test (see page 211) and then focus on the detailed sections pertinent to your lowest score. This test will highlight the areas in which you may tend to erect barriers between yourself and a loved one.

2. If you're simply interested in learning more about how couples stay happy in the long-term, you may want to read *Choose to Be Happily Married* from start to finish. Each chapter includes stories about real people. Also, like our personalities, many of the twenty-five issues discussed in the chapters are interconnected and complex. By exploring the Turning Points sequentially, you can achieve a panoramic view of how to remain satisfied *within* an imperfect love.

However you approach *Choose to Be Happily Married,* this is a book that can become a life tool to examine and re-examine as you gather experiences. Jean-Paul Sartre, in his classic book *Existential Psychoanalysis,* tells us that we *are* the choices we make. It is the actions of our life that determine ultimately who we are. The rest of this book is devoted to developing that idea. Finding—and keeping—real, adult contentment is a skill like any other, requiring technique and practice. I wish you luck and wise intention as you begin your journey.

Part I
Flexibility

Chapter 1

RESPONSIVE VERSUS REACTIVE
*Choosing to Be Receptive in a Moment
of Stress*

Each Turning Point you encounter in this book has as its under-
pinnings this first choice: responsive versus reactive. This is the
decision you must make—in a moment of stress—to act in a
way that reflects a lifetime of hard-won adult wisdom rather
than a habitual reflex originating in childhood. Once you
understand this fundamental choice and how it colors your intimate relationship, you will have a solid foundation for building
a lasting love.

HOW LOVE AFFECTS YOUR LIFE

When you fall in love, you hear about "two becoming one," the power of love as a force that heals any conflict. You look down at your linked hands on the third date and ponder the perfection: *I will never grow tired of this person. He was made for me.* As true as this may seem, he was also made *from* somewhere—a set of parents, siblings, and experiences that coalesced to create this complex individual. Uniqueness is part of the magic of being human, and when you meet that person whose individuality complements your own distinctive traits, it feels like a miracle. And it is. However, time compels you to take a closer look. Differences will eventually bubble up from the depths, inevitable as air.

Helen Fisher, in her seminal work *Why We Love,* explains physical correlations to changes in human feelings and speaks about the three core brain systems for mating and reproduction: lust—beginning chemistry (the sex drive or libido); romantic attraction—lasting up to two years (romantic love); and ultimately attachment (union with a long-term partner). This book defines the twenty-five elements that determine the quality of the experience during the attachment stage.

Within attachment, love becomes not a separate force existing outside of you—some half-dressed cupid madly searching his pockets for more arrows—but rather a shared bond it is your job to protect, even in the face of disagreements. Moments of empathic disconnect, in which you are unable to really "get" where your partner is coming from, are the natural products of human attachment. When faced with inevitable discord, you have a choice: you can counter with fury, frustration, impatience, and disdain—all of which are reactive behaviors. Or, you can respond by trying to put yourself in your partner's shoes through emotional control, serenity, and tolerance, as well as the desire to learn something new. All are responsive behaviors. This fundamental decision can, over time, make the difference between lasting love, in which boundaries are established, and affection that is chipped away by barriers built with the mortar of reactivity.

Nevertheless, anyone who has ever been faced with a partner's backseat driving, lateness, wet towel on the floor, overspending, or five drinks at dinner knows that the easier path—a reactive reflex—often feels like the only choice. After all, aren't you the victim of this outrageous behavior? Why should *you* be the bigger person? The answer: you only have the power to alter your own conduct, and this act may influence positive change.

YOU CAN ONLY CHANGE YOURSELF

Imagine that for over a decade you and your wife have had a transparent financial arrangement. This system has worked; money is rarely a source of angst. One Tuesday you get a call from the bank saying the account ending in 1234 is overdrawn, and could you confirm some purchases? You don't recognize the account number, but listen as she lists the vendors: Macy's tops the inventory with a $1,500 purchase. The teller continues reading as your confusion lifts and is replaced by rage. Your wife apparently has a secret account from which she primarily buys clothes and jewelry.

You have two hours left in the workday to make a decision that could affect your marriage dramatically. You can barely contain the rising feelings of betrayal. You consider how hard you work to save money—which she apparently spends freely—and then remember generous gifts you have bought her. She could have just bought them herself—probably would have preferred to!

You are in such a state by the time she walks in the door that you shove some paperwork off the table, where it falls at her feet. "You lying bitch!" you scream, and storm off to brood. The week-long argument that this declaration kicks off leaves little room for rational discussion. Guilt and anger fill your home, and it will take work to rebuild the connection that was severed—by her behavior and yours. So, what could you have done differently? What would be the responsive choice that would sustain your love during this difficult revelation?

CHOOSING TO BE RESPONSIVE

First, there is no denying that this situation is difficult. She has made her own unfortunate choice by a lie of omission. However, no amount of recrimination is going to change that fact. What's done is done. The question is why it was done, and how you can move on. Let's go back to the dining room. Your wife walks in to find you sitting alone. You invite her to join you and describe your conversation with the bank representative. She immediately begins to cry. You take a deep breath and say, "I feel angry and betrayed, but I really want to understand this." This simple opening gives her the space to explain. The connection is not severed; a line of communication remains open despite the pain. Perhaps her secret account was due to never having enough as a child and wanting a sense of total control over something that was all hers. Maybe she only deposited cash from her side projects to fund the account. Whatever her rationale, by approaching the problem with thoughtful intention, the two of you can maintain your connection while mending this conflict.

When people react, it is usually driven by unresolved experiences. As children, we may have watched our parents duke it out, through yelling, silence, sarcasm, or even violence. We have carried these lessons with us. Now, when we feel threatened or hurt, our instinct is to revert to our original experiences with discord. At five years old, the only thing we knew to do was react unthinkingly. Tantrums and holding our breath until we were blue were par for the course for some. But, now, at ages thirty-five, forty, or sixty, we have a choice: we can take a cleansing breath (or two or twenty), detach from our past, and see the world through adult eyes, a perspective that opens a window into the complexity of other people's motivations.

SALLY AND DON

Often, one reactive event—a slammed phone, a huffy exit—can open a door to hidden emotional fissures. Such was the case with Sally and Don, a couple who have persevered despite the difficulties of raising three children, one of whom is disabled, on a single income. Don, with encouragement from his wife and another couples' therapist, became a member of one of my groups to augment the work they were already doing to improve the quality of their relationship. But first some background:

Sally and their oldest son, Adam—now fourteen—had a ritual of heading down the block to Starbucks for a daily treat. One particular day, they had put off their coffee visit until evening, forgetting that Adam's drum teacher was scheduled for a lesson then. Don was annoyed as he sat with the scruffy teacher awaiting their return, but impatience transformed into a familiar sense of deep frustration when Sally's cell phone sent him straight to voice mail.

Twenty minutes later, they heard the familiar jangle of keys at the door. Apologies were made, and everything was sorted out. But Don couldn't let it go.

DON STANDS AT A CROSSROADS

When you feel you've been wronged, you have options:

1. Make sure that the other person understands your position.
2. React in any number of destructive ways: silent brooding, yelling, or passive aggressive behavior.
3. Notice what is bothering you and keep it to yourself while exploring the other person's perspective. Once you recognize his or her viewpoint, you can build a bridge from your side to your partner's through discussion.

What would you do? Can you envision a scene from your life when you were at this type of crossroads?

As you will see, Don chose the second alternative: to react from his aggrieved outlook.

Later that night, as Sally was getting the kids water from the kitchen, Don stood blocking her path, cell phone in hand. "I bought you this specifically to avoid this evening's inconvenience," he hissed, tossing the phone carelessly. It clattered onto the granite countertop. "When I call and it goes directly to voice mail, I know that you are just ignoring me. You probably have it programmed somehow so that my calls don't even ring."

Sally stood frozen, not believing the amount of suspicion this minor incident had stirred up. What was lying beneath Don's disproportionate reaction? She suddenly pushed past him, got the spare sheets out of the closet, and began making up the couch. *God*, she thought, *I assumed I had three needy kids, but apparently I have four.*

THE FALLOUT

Although it is repeated everywhere, from books to talk shows to your grandmother's words of wisdom, the mantra "never go to bed angry" is simplistic and sometimes unrealistic. As Sally demonstrates, it can be impossible, in a difficult moment, to do the intimate listening required to find an empathic connection between you and your partner. (See Chapter 16 for more about the art of intimate listening.) If you find yourself in this position, say something like, "We agree to disagree for now, but let's make a date to find out why we are seeing things so differently." This gives your relationship the benefit of the doubt that you can eventually figure it out, and it provides space so that you can both listen to each other's experience of what happened.

(Of course, sleeping separately is also reactive and a prescription for dismantling a trusting love. Using sex as a tool for power is a no-no if lasting affection is your goal. When it comes to consensual lovemaking, any sex is good for a couple. Never turn it down—when it's gone you will regret the opportunities you missed not taking advantage of this comforting way to reconnect. But even if sex is not in the offing, the act of sleeping in the same space can soften the dynamic, building a thread—however fragile—of intimacy.)

Don's choice to lash out at Sally—to be reactive rather than responsive—caused a tense couple of days. Sally's feelings of confusion surrounding this event added to her customary sense of being overwhelmed by her life. Don's accusatory reaction left him feeling trapped by his own anger, bereft at his inability to re-establish a connection to his wife.

Accusing the other is a recipe for isolated self-entrapment, which will be discussed in more detail in Chapter 11, Taking Responsibility versus Blame. For now, notice how Don's decision to blame his wife literally led to isolation. His night alone in their bed—usually a refuge to rediscover intimacy—lasted an eternity, the evening's events playing in an unending loop in his mind.

AN ENCOUNTER WITH AN OUTSIDER'S PERSPECTIVE CHANGES THE GAME

In group therapy the next day, which Don relied upon as a safe haven in which to discuss his marital strife, one of the members spoke up after hearing Don's story: "What if Sally wasn't avoiding just your calls, Don, but all calls? I know when I've had it at the end of the day, sometimes I turn off my cell phone."

Another woman concurred: "Yeah, I love my cell phone when I need to make a call, but I don't always have it on or it would drive me crazy." From this detached vantage point, Don was finally able to envision that the cell phone being turned off could possibly mean something other than "Sally doesn't give a damn about me."

Don recognized that a sense of helplessness and distance from his wife caused him to lash out in desperation for a bond, even if it came about through conflict. But, his tactic hadn't worked. Sally was more distant than ever, distracted and terse in their moments alone—even in their lovemaking.

DON'T GIVE IN TO DESPERATION

Feeling helpless can lead to desperation. If you act desperate, then you become needy, dependent, and insatiable—surefire ways to isolate your partner. Of course, in this childlike state, reactivity is the obvious option. In that instant, you are two years old again, ready to lie down in the middle of the sidewalk and wail in utter despair, which translates to "Love me! Pay attention to me! Be my everything!"

How do you avoid these worrisome reactions? Try self-soothing. Remind yourself that this will pass, that you have had many good moments with your partner and that they will come again. Do not give in to feeling that all is lost. That is never true unless you make it true.

Up until this point, Don had stubbornly hung on to his reactive behavior, actions and words arising from a dread of being invisible and the butt of other people's frustrations, as he had felt growing up. It was time for Don to make the choice to approach his wife in a responsive manner.

A CONNECTING RESPONSE

The next day when he called Sally and was sent to voice mail, he could feel his face get hot. But he took a deep breath, acknowledged his negative emotions, and allowed them to pass. Maybe not everything was about him, after all. Trying for levity, he left a message about taking the car to their long-winded mechanic that he knew Sally would find funny.

Later, at home, they were having a pleasant family meal when Don mentioned casually that a friend of his had a theory about cell phones: that they are a tool to make our lives less complicated, not more, and that we shouldn't become victims of technology.

Here, Don demonstrated the power of creating a safe space. This opening allowed Sally room to explain her take on it. "I couldn't agree more. Sometimes I have to turn it off to save my sanity," she laughed. The subject soon turned to the kids' school day, but Sally ran her hand lightly across his back on her way to the kitchen, a private signal for later intimacy.

Don's thoughtful, responsive choice highlights the fact that it is only through changing ourselves can we hope to alter the emotional environment between two people. He is learning to subvert his reflexive impulse into more constructive responses, giving Sally a chance to wrap him inside her love instead of resenting his neediness.

Every successful relationship is its own unique dance—a choreography that works due to the comfortable boundaries each person puts in place. These boundaries allow you to retain your independence even as you move through life with another person. Responsive behavior supports boundaries, upholding your connection with a loved one while allowing room for limitations and mistakes.

Reactive behavior, on the other hand, erects barriers. The dance ends as you stumble over the other's feet or sever the connection by walking away. When conflict arises, reactions such as instantaneous anger or unyielding silence construct a barrier that's difficult to break down. It's like a self-built prison—each person stands in it, unaware that they hold the key to let themselves out.

It is easy to see this Turning Point at work in the world. Anger, xenophobia, ignorance, and a thirst for power have blazed their own reactive path through poor, war-torn countries—and even the United States. This thoughtless zeal has taken a literal toll on human lives. As well, like a child screaming for a toy, our need-it-now consumerism has put our planet in peril. How can we shape our lives in such a way as to affect change? If each of us lives with thoughtful intention—first toward our partner, then family, community, and the world— these small steps could result in the beginning of a happier existence for all.

Chapter 2

GOOD JUDGMENT VERSUS CRITICAL JUDGMENT

Making Room for Another's Beliefs

Critical judgment—imposing one's strict belief system on another—is a worldwide epidemic. Whether the subject is politics, religion, sports, fashion, or sexuality, a my-way-or-the-highway approach has become *de rigueur*. Many people place a significant emphasis on being intellectually inflexible. Having an uncompromising opinion connotes strength and demands respect at dinner parties and on the cable news shows—or so we are taught by contemporary culture. However, when it comes to intimate relationships, this approach can have negative repercussions.

YOU ARE WHAT YOU BELIEVE

Very few people—including siblings—grow up with identical belief systems. For this reason, when you meet someone and fall in love, there will always be adjustments: The puzzle pieces *almost* fit, yet you each have to shift one way or another, giving an inch, taking an inch. As anyone who has ever moved in with a lover can attest, this process can be both frustrating and hilarious: *Who taught him to load the dishes like that? She compulsively washes the sheets every Tuesday!*

We all have beliefs that are fundamental to who we are and how we operate in the world. These convictions—when adhered to tightly and forced upon others—can erode even the most solid bond. In particular, strict moral codes and rigid lifestyle choices may trigger critically judgmental behavior. When two people each think that their own answer is the *one* correct answer—and that answer is poles apart from the partner's—a stalemate ensues. The connection is broken.

It often comes to pass that people are most passionate when debating questions that have an element of subjectivity to them—from universal mysteries such as religion to ever-changing social issues such as sexual orientation and public decorum. These make us yell all the more loudly, as it is difficult to arrive at the "truth." But, as important as it is to hold an opinion on how to behave and in whose God we should believe or not believe, it is equally as important to respect your lover's right to do the same.

Like every barrier-building choice you will encounter in this book, being critically judgmental is a result of early experiences that continue to shadow your life. In childhood, you were an empty vessel, eager to be filled by the lessons your parents and teachers imparted. You took comfort in being "good"; you wanted to please your caregivers, earn their love. Half a lifetime later, you may find that some of the teachings about the "right" way to live have tenacious sticking power. And these are probably the things you fight about, the ones upon which you insist your partner agree.

THE IMPORTANCE OF BEING FLEXIBLE

It is often surprising which beliefs end up sticking with you the most. It is easy to imagine the fireworks ensuing should an evangelical Christian decide to marry a staunch atheist. But consider Jane, who grew up in a formal Southern family. When she married Jim, he already had three teenage sons from his first marriage. Jane turned a critical eye on Jim's kids, with their ripped shorts and oversized T-shirts. They offended her sense of how "proper" boys should dress. She insisted that the boys wear collared shirts—even when playing outside, biking, and skateboarding. Jim tried reasoning with her. His boys were rough-and-tumble and it would be a battle to force them into polo shirts at every moment of the day. Jane's critical judgment of his children's clothing choices had at its root a long-held idea about propriety that she learned from her mother. Her stubbornness about what Jim viewed as a silly, inconsequential thing made him question their budding marriage.

The minute you think you have the *only* answer, you build a barrier between your loved one and yourself. Instead, exercise good judgment and allow room for another's perspective and opinions. This is not to say that you should throw your own moral or social compasses out the window. Rather, listen to your partner's differing views with respect and humbly agree that no one has all the answers. Imagine nightly dinner at the home of Democrat Maria Shriver and her Republican governor husband. You can bet there are some diverse opinions in that household! But you can also guess that given their long partnership, they approach the other's differences with deference and humor. This ability to be mentally flexible—to listen rather than dictatorially impart—is one of the keys to lasting love.

JENNIFER AND JEFF

Jennifer's friends joke that she is not shy about giving her opinion on any number of topics. In fact, many of them know to expect a storm of unsolicited advice, should they bring up their horrid mother-in-law or troubled teen over lunch. Good judgment would entail listening with compassion and offering few unasked-for suggestions. But Jennifer, a petite office manager, means well, so her friends forgive her occasional inclination to be insufferably opinionated. However, it is another matter entirely for her husband, Jeff.

The moral path that Jennifer feels is correct is a narrow one. Her belief system tills fertile ground for the critical judgment she imposes on her husband daily. Feeling her criticisms are justified, Jennifer says exactly what is on her mind, not pausing to edit her words or consider how they will affect her mate. Jeff, a soft-spoken computer analyst, has learned to tune her out most of the time, only occasionally snapping back in anger. Even when he attempts to explain himself, he feels that Jennifer does not listen to his justifications, since she is so entrenched in her point of view. After twenty years of marriage, Jennifer and Jeff have steadily built a barrier between themselves—she with her critical judgment and he with his retaliatory withdrawal.

When you feel judged, your instinct may be to rebel, withdraw, or reject. In fact, offering lasting love and understanding in this situation may feel counterintuitive. However, it is empathy—compassionately considering how and why the other person feels strongly about something—that builds a bridge and leads to a more fertile relationship. If you don't understand your partner's opinion, try to explore his position with an open mind. It takes intimate listening skills to create a safe space in which another can open up. Once you discover the reason for his passion you can acknowledge your understanding of where he is coming from and choose either to be influenced or to hold on to your own view.

Jennifer's insistence on voicing her opinion arises from a childhood ensconced in impermeable silence: Children were seen and not heard. When Jennifer was eight, her uncle overstepped her sexual boundaries and there was no one for her to turn to, no one who would listen. As a result, she made a promise to herself during adolescence to never be silent, to always be heard no matter what the cost. Now, it was taking a toll on her marriage.

JENNIFER ERUPTS

After dinner one night, Jennifer and Jeff were lingering at the table, discussing their son's recent wedding. Jeff made an offhand remark about their daughter-in-law's large breasts. He was trying to be funny and assumed Jennifer would have to be blind not to have noticed the girl's ample attributes. She just stared at him, revulsion building. He could feel her mood shift darkly as she rose from the table. "How disgusting! Your own daughter-in-law! What are you—a pervert?" she said, storming out of the room.

What could Jennifer have done in this situation to exercise good judgment rather than become critically judgmental? How could she have approached Jeff's comment in a more trusting manner, even if she was not sure whether her husband was insensitive or truly acting perverse? It is easy to understand Jennifer's instantaneous reaction, given her childhood experiences. But, as an adult, she has the power to make a conscious choice: She could revel in her righteous anger or take a deep breath and choose to respond with thoughtful intention. For instance, she could have said, "She is a pretty girl, but listen, Jeff: You know my history, so understand that sexual comments about family—however innocent they may seem to you—make me uncomfortable." An example of good judgment, this nonaccusatory response would have allowed Jennifer to express her discomfort, thus building a boundary instead of erecting a barrier. It also would have given Jeff the space to sensitively select his next move, perhaps apologizing to his wife with less defensive anger.

CHOOSE LOVE OVER ALIENATION

Often, your growth as an adult necessitates giving up early vows to yourself. Rather than viewing a change of heart as a submersion of a fundamental aspect of your identity, you could opt to see that the worldview you held when you were young was based on limited knowledge. If you gain comfort with flexibility, you'll enjoy more opportunities for constructive experiences. After all, your life circumstances have changed since you were a child, so it's okay for your views to change, too.

Jennifer—stubbornly holding on to a belief system formed as a preteen—is interfering with her choices by refusing to re-evaluate her childhood promise to herself. To her, the world is neatly divided into two categories: your way or my way. There is comfort in living like this, the sense of satisfaction of being right at the expense of someone else being wrong. This consolation is fleeting, however, especially as her criticisms continue to alienate those she loves the most. Jeff and others in her life could eventually grow weary of being judged, and these relationships may falter. Jennifer *thought* her current choice was being heard versus keeping quiet, but the choice was actually being critical versus exercising good judgment and finding a bridge-building path toward mutual understanding and acceptance.

NAGGING: CRITICAL JUDGMENT'S EVERYDAY DISGUISE

The most common form of critical judgment—nagging—is one we are all familiar with, as either perpetrator or recipient. A staple of modern domesticity, this type of harassment may seem mundane, but over time it can cause cracks in the foundation of a happy home. The famous American thinker William James once said, "The art of being wise is the art of knowing what to overlook." Nagging is choosing to not overlook *anything*.

NAGGING GIVES YOU A FALSE SENSE OF CONTROL

It is often the case that pestering arises out of a feeling of helplessness—a lack of control over your shared environment with another. *If he hasn't walked the dog, fixed the car, found a job. . . .*

Well, I'll just nag him until he does. Nagging is critical—and few people react to criticism with positive action. A better choice is to sit down with your partner, hold her hand, look in her eyes and ask: "Do you know any way that I could help you to clear your desk? The clutter disturbs my tranquility when I want to go to sleep." She may respond by contemplating why the cluttered desk—or whatever it is—perpetually bothers you and then, if she sees her behavior as insensitive, comply or ask for your assistance.

Of course, there will be instances where you don't agree that a loved one's request is necessary. Imagine that your partner feels if there are just a few dishes in the sink, they should be hand-washed rather than loaded in the dishwasher. If you disagree, you can firmly tell him, "I do not agree and I wish to use the dishwasher instead. It saves time and water, too. And I prefer not to be nagged about my decision." If the nagging continues, have compassion and a bit of patience—it may be a way to let off steam if he is anxious. If you know he's dreading a big presentation at work the following day, let it go, knowing his micromanagement of your dishwashing is likely an aberration.

HOW TO COMBAT NAGGING

If your energy level is different from your partner's and you perceive him as lazy, you may find it difficult not to nag. But remember, nagging is a sign of your impotence. Empower yourself by a daily reminder of why you chose your partner. Write a list of reasons. Some examples on that inventory could be that he is kind; gave you a baby; is funny, playful, refreshing, and not uptight; you have good chemistry and the same basic values; and so on. Put it on your mirror, the refrigerator, your closet. Use *this* as a reminder of your power to appreciate who he is.

IT'S ALL ABOUT TOLERANCE

Critical judgment annihilates relationships—it is a quintessential barrier-building behavior. Upholding a strong connection with your partner is an ongoing endeavor that requires vigilance—a consistent self-awareness that prevents a slide into the easy trap of derogatory conclusions. We hold the ones closest to us to high standards, but at the same time this proximity means we are acutely aware of their faults and foibles, making criticism tempting.

This is a two-way street, however, and it can be helpful to recall that you are imperfect as well. Of course, the less accepting you are of your own imperfections, the less you will be of your partner's. Self-criticism stems from your early experiences. You can't wipe out the original patterning or unconscious drives. However, you can stand vigilantly on guard to be aware of when the past is flooding the present. During those times, self-observation will help to quiet your mind and give you the opportunity to think more clearly about whether you are choosing to be critically judgmental or not.

On this journey of lifelong love, it is essential that after you determine what bothers you about your partner or yourself, you then select what is important to voice. Giving feedback that can strengthen your partner's functioning makes you a valuable mate; overlooking the rest makes you a lovable companion.

Chapter 3

EXPRESSING YOUR TRUE SELF VERSUS CONFORMING TO A ROLE
Being Yourself Even as Roles Shift

Throughout our twenties, we are challenged by the demands of new and unfamiliar experiences. This is a supple developmental stage where the choices seem endless: We are young workers or students, single or attached, moving from town to city or vice versa, among a thousand other options. We are seekers, trying to find roles that will lead to contentment. The nature of this challenge—during this time and throughout our lives—is the willingness to discover how to incorporate our authentic selves into our roles as they expand and grow with changing circumstances.

Once we discover what we want to pursue, we then need to figure out how. This is usually the task of the next decade. By our mid-thirties, we have either settled on the big decisions or know what we want and are in hot pursuit. We have learned some hard-won lessons, and we likely have adjusted to the roles we initially chose, or have discarded them for a better fit. Within both of these early stages, change is an accepted constant.

WHEN YOUR ROLES BECOME MURKY

Once you hit your forties and beyond, you face a different choice, composed of three possibilities:

1. You overthrow your original roles.
2. You remain stuck in a static life of quiet desperation.
3. You challenge yourself to expand the boundaries of the roles you selected earlier to fit with your emerging self.

It is a developmental inevitability that this stage challenges you both internally and externally. Imagine you begin to feel restricted or not stimulated by your current love and/or work life. In a burst of frustration, you shatter your known universe with all the usual midlife crisis harbingers: having an affair, buying needless toys, gaining or losing a massive amount of weight, fighting with bosses or colleagues—even quitting your job or selling or closing your business. Or, conversely, you dig your heels into the sand and, despite claustrophobic feelings, become fearful of change, clinging to the known with a renewed intensity.

No matter what your comfort zone is, the outside world changes, and the choice to either reactively break out of an established role (because of feeling trapped) or burrow down into it (due to a fear of change) can have negative consequences. Alternatively, searching for a *constructive* way to grow and expand within your already established roles may provide a path toward continued challenge and ultimately, fulfillment—or it may show you through trial and error that moving on is the fitting course.

For example, imagine you become a firefighter, get married, and have two children. These roles (firefighter, spouse, parent) have the potential to broaden, stretching to accommodate an emerging self. Perhaps you receive a promotion, which gives you more professional responsibilities. Or, you develop a new set of skills to be an effective parent of teenage children. Rising to these occasions can provide a renewed sense of fulfillment. Should your partner do the same, you both will develop and mature. A dynamic life—albeit with good times and bad—follows.

Inflexibility as roles shift has a potentially disastrous outcome: stagnation. Promotions dwindle without new job skills, teenagers become miserable, and marriage lifeless. If you fail to vary your perspective as your life evolves, you become stuck. Depending on your partner's evolution, this immovable place will either tear you apart or leave you trapped together in your cocoon.

CARIN AND SAM

January is the toughest month for Carin and Sam, parents to Fred and Andrew, both of whom are pursuing careers abroad and have families of their own. Christmas now over, grandchildren gone, Carin sinks into an annual depression, bemoaning the fact that "everyone" has moved far away. When she was growing up, it would have never occurred to her to venture abroad for an opportunity. She spent her 1950s childhood baking cookies with grandma and running lemonade stands with her cousins. It seems unfair to Carin that she cannot replicate that situation with her sons and grandchildren. After all those years raising her family, her role as a mother feels like an empty shell.

Sam, on the other hand, is proud that his boys ventured out to find their own path, as he did. "Why can't we just be happy, the two of us?" Sam asks Carin one day.

"Happy with maybe one phone call a week, if that? Janice's girls live one town over; she sees them for brunch after church and for shopping during the week. Hard to have that with an ocean between us and our children," Carin blurts out.

"It's the natural way of things, damn it. Kids leave the nest," Sam says, frustrated by her refusal to make the best of the situation. *It's not my fault!* he thinks. But Sam feels guilty. Fred and Andrew are much more likely to spontaneously call Sam's office than to phone home. Both sons have careers that dovetail into their father's real estate interests and, more important, Sam doesn't begin each conversation with, "Well, hello, stranger," or the cringe-inducing, "It wouldn't kill you to call home once in a while."

If life is a river, Carin is stuck midstream, letting time—and the prospect of happiness—flow by. She hopes that if she refuses to budge, the role she had when her children were young will re-present itself. After all, it was a job—stay-at-home mom—at which she excelled. She is still willing to be that mom for them, so the fact that they no longer need her fills her with a sense of betrayal, followed by guilt over being selfish. What she does not want to accept is that this role no longer exists. Hints of this loss create a feeling of despair that leaks into every aspect of her life—especially her marriage.

STUCK TOGETHER

One sign that you may be inflexible or trapped in a role is if you feel resentment toward those in your life who live differently from the implicit bargain that you had with them. In this case, the unstated bargain was that Sam would remain fixed with Carin in her all-consuming role as parent, now grandparent—that he would feel betrayed by their sons' "abandonment" as well. Now, as Sam floats on with the current, changing with his shifting circumstances, the breach between him and his wife is widening. What once was a strong bond built over years of shared experience raising their children is now a sore spot. In the past, discussing the children was a primary conversational topic; now dinners are fraught with silence, as neither wants to broach this thorny subject. To happily remain together, Carin must choose to release her established role in exchange for one in which she learns to nurture in new ways. Expanding her "Mother" role to fit her current situation will foster a new beginning with Sam.

EMBRACING CHANGE

The best tool for breaking free of fixed patterns is to find a new passion. For some it is going deeper into religion, finding a charity that speaks to you, learning a sport, getting a degree at a continuing education university, learning yoga or tango—anything fresh that engages unused parts of your brain.

Not long after Carin and Sam's stilted conversation, Carin's childhood friend, Shelley, reached out to her. This woman had cared for a daughter with cystic fibrosis, who died at age twenty. Shelley was left with an endless number of hours in which to mourn. She decided to become productive again by volunteering and reconnecting with people she neglected during her daughter's illness. After spending time with Shelley, Carin realized how lucky she was to have a family separated solely by miles. She began to see that her focus on what used to be was draining her present circumstances of its full potential: the freedom to find creative alternatives within her current roles as mother, grandmother, friend, and wife.

Carin's increasing willingness to accept her boys' choices opened up the space for a renewed bond with her husband. With tension lessening, they began looking for shared interests, new ways to bring them into the present. Carin's role as Sam's wife expanded to being his bridge partner and co-birdwatcher. Sam's guilt lessened in proportion to Carin's diminishing focus on the children's distance. He was no longer secretive about Fred and Andrew's calls. In fact, from time to time he would conference their mother in just to say hello. Carin's evolving openness is providing the flexibility that acknowledges changing circumstances and people, leading to more satisfying connections.

UNDERSTANDING CHANGES OVER A LIFETIME

Marriages and long-term partnerships are challenging for the obvious reason that the person we met five, ten, or twenty years ago is now a new and often different version of the original. I often hear patients complain to each other, "I don't even know you anymore!" This implies that one has moved forward in his or her respective role, leaving the other behind in a cloud of uncertainty. One person feels betrayed: *How could she change?* The better question would be,

How can I understand this change? Appreciating how your partner re-creates his roles can help you see the world through his eyes, facilitating mutual understanding. It can also lead to a fascinating, long-term partnership where new discoveries about your partner as well as yourself are forever emerging.

THE CHALLENGING CHILD YEARS

This issue of expanding your roles to fit who you are and what you want out of life is especially difficult for young families. The demands of raising children can devolve into quarrels over long-held, engrained beliefs about gender. Even in the best of circumstances, in which each partner is living within the role he or she chooses, such as co-earner, stay-at-home mom or dad, or some combination thereof, most couples with kids will agree that established roles often expand and contract without notice. The mom who works at the office all day wonders why she is still awake at 1 A.M. baking cookies for little Sammy's class. *Weren't these types of responsibilities supposed to be shared?* she fumes, as her husband—oblivious to the demands of the PTA—dreams on.

There are limits to expanding your roles. Reaching a breaking point as the do-it-all mom or dad is a common occurrence and can result in anger, burnout, and an inability to enjoy the fleeting years of having young children. Worse, it can lead to disharmony within a couple that threatens the very partnership a burgeoning family is based on. Despite the myriad books written about this subject, the only true consensus is that this stage of life involves difficult decision-making. It's crucial to communicate and support each other as you shift and grow.

Very often, when stretched to the limit, you build resentment toward your partner. You project the dark feeling inside of yourself onto him. You see him as selfish, lazy, clueless, or cheap. At this moment of disconnect it is better to be suspicious of the black picture you have painted, move to clear your mind, and then with a mindset of benefit of the doubt, check in with how your partner sees the same situation. Also, to appreciate your mutual joy and sacrifice, carve out time together to increase your possibility of happiness. "Date Night" may sound trite, but there are few remedies more healing than being together outside the realm of daily demands.

Ideally, throughout the partnership journey, your roles expand to take advantage of life's potential opportunities. The choice is yours: to remain stuck, watching from the sidelines, or to embrace your own and your lover's growing and shifting identities, thus enriching your love. Lately I have been asking couples who have been together for more than thirty years how many marriages they have had so far. After a moment of confusion, they understand that I mean marriages with the same person. Couples are forever in flux. Perhaps without even being consciously aware of it, all people who succeed in maintaining long-term relationships make the choice of flexibility over rigidity—the willingness to survive and go with the flow even if the river of their lives takes them in a completely unplanned for—and perhaps initially unwished for—direction. Flexibility ensures a challenging, yet dynamic, love experience.

Chapter 4

AUTONOMY VERSUS ISOLATION

Standing Up for Yourself Without Isolating Your Partner

Anyone with a craving for autonomy will be familiar with the heady, heart-pumping feeling of a fresh start: getting off the bus in a new city; transforming a long-held identity of being the "shy" girl or the "fat" kid; playing by no one's rules but your own. In a cloud of dust, we leave behind the shame of adolescent missteps, the overbearing mommy or daddy who would swallow us alive with their love. This exhilarating emotion of leaving the known for the unknown feels pioneering. We become self-sufficient, accountable to no one.

KEEPING ISOLATION AT BAY

The independence that accompanies the choice to be autonomous—whether alone or within a romantic relationship—is an expression of adult self-reliance. While love creates a shared entity, retaining separateness maintains the distinctive characteristics that define you. Expressing this can be as simple as a weekly guys- or girls-only poker night or a weekend trip with a friend. Taking private time to pursue interests provides breathing room, and increases vibrancy within a couple.

But the grab for autonomy can gain momentum and, without notice, morph into isolation, a state that thwarts happiness. What does independence mean to you? Are you fleeing to escape feeling trapped? Are you becoming rigid? Inflexibility is a defense born out of a fear that if you let your guard down you will revert to some previous version of yourself, such as the boy no one wants to sit next to in the lunchroom, or mommy's best companion. Autonomy, which becomes a protection against vulnerability, runs the risk of producing rigidity when you go to extremes to isolate yourself from those around you. Keeping love at arm's length by refusing to emotionally engage, or physically leaving those closest to you in the name of "freedom" and "independence," negates the possibility of love's give-and-take. In the case of autonomy, the more we crave it, the greater the possibility of isolation.

But, what's so negative about isolation? Being alone means freedom from compromise, the opportunity to do what you want, when you want. Ask any young parent what he or she wouldn't give for a few "isolating" hours to read a novel or take a walk! The ability to enjoy your own company is part of becoming an actualized adult. So, why is isolation un-applauded? Since we are social animals, even the most self-sufficient among us will eventually head down to the local coffee shop to ease his creeping feeling of loneliness. In a romantic relationship, however, isolation builds a barrier of silent absence. You may be happy doing your own thing, but if your loved one is left wanting and waiting, this could lead to the relationship's demise. Isolation is harmful if your actions unintentionally cut off another. Read what happened to Irene and Thomas in their search for autonomy.

IRENE AND THOMAS

From an outsider's perspective, Irene had gotten exactly what she wanted: a husband and four kids, and a life out west near the Rockies, where al fresco adventure was just outside her door. So why did she feel as if a cloud had hung over her happiness for the majority of her marriage? Twenty years before, when she and Thomas left their East Coast families, the promise of freedom brought their love to a heightened level. They would carve out a life for themselves, away from his mother "popping in" at their apartment unannounced, and her father, who had never warmed up to the new man in his daughter's life. This "mommy's boy" and "daddy's girl" wanted a fresh start!

Thomas especially enjoyed their autonomy. In fact, he became so accustomed to following his own beat that he was increasingly absent from their burgeoning family. Fifteen years and four kids later, Thomas spent most of his time playing in his band and traveling for work, leaving Irene to be the primary parent . . . and solitary partner. Thomas's absence was gradual. Irene rarely voiced her creeping loneliness. After all, she had always admired his independent spirit.

OVERCOMING THOMAS'S ISOLATION

Early in his adulthood, Thomas had vowed to prevent the outcome he most feared: his tendency to become "pussy-whipped," just as he had been a "momma's boy" growing up. To his mind, the best way to resist this feminine gravitational pull was absence. But what had begun as a quest for autonomy all those years ago had turned into abandoning Irene in their marriage. Thomas was relatively content with the structure of the relationship. His need

for independence was stronger than his desire to be Irene's ultimate, all-the-time lover. Irene felt this disconnect acutely.

Soon after their oldest two children left home—one for college
back east and one to start a business—Irene was bereft. The house
was only half as noisy. With just the two youngest at home, and
Thomas pursuing his own interests, Irene felt the isolation more
than ever. Taking a courageous step, she decided to join a women's
drumming group to meet new people. The women she encountered there were mostly older, maternal, with a hippy, free-spirit
vibe. Taking Irene into their fold, she was adored, a darling little
girl again. She was inspired for the first time in years.

These friendships and new activities—including turning
drumming into a business as a part-time teacher—allowed her to
gain footing in her marriage. It also forced Thomas to do more
childcare in the wake of Irene's pursuits, meaning his music mostly
took place at home or not at all. This correction of a decades-long
imbalance shook up the tacit agreement that had carved scars into
their marriage.

IRENE OPENS UP

Irene's new confidence propelled her to open up about her
feelings of loneliness. Thomas was dumbfounded that she felt
he had abandoned her. From his perspective, he was supporting
them so she could do what she wanted: be a stay-at-home mom.
It took time for him to own that his "vow" had transformed his
passion for independence into the darker realm of isolating his
wife. Thomas eventually acknowledged that in seeking autonomy, he unintentionally took his lust for independence too far.
In dealing with his fear of losing his identity, which was rooted
in his too-close relationship with his mother, he had abandoned
his wife.

To ensure that lasting love will be part of the second half of
their lives, Irene and Thomas's challenge is to find a communication path. Thomas can dial back his tendency to float off by spend-

ing time with his wife. Irene can support his pursuit of music and work, while sharing her secret emotional life. Checking in with each other will be key for this couple.

HOW TO KNOW IF YOU'RE ISOLATING ANOTHER

There are some signs to look out for if you suspect you are isolating your partner. Consider these:

- If neither you nor your partner often initiates private conversations, there is a possibility that one or both of you feel isolated from the other. With little personal exchange, your partner may feel isolated even if you are sleeping in the same bed nightly, sharing the bathroom, toothpaste, and water glass.

- If, when you are together, your partner is dreamy, quiet, irritable, angry, or maudlin, check to find out whether you have anything to do with this joyless mood. Even if he insists it has nothing to do with you, just paying attention, showing curiosity, and making space may help accomplish your goal of reducing loneliness. He may not need to share what is bothering him. That is his privilege. But you have offered the security of a receptive ear poised to listen when he is ready.

MOTIVATIONS FOR ISOLATION

Fear of conflict is a primary reason some people become isolated. This phenomenon is prevalent among my single clients who—though they claim to be searching for love—have built elaborate designs to avoid it. Being unhappily alone is easier than risking the conflict and compromise that love invariably brings. So, in a classic "Three Little Pigs" scenario, they build a sturdy brick house in order to keep out the big bad wolf. Alone in the dark they sit, safe and miserable, reinforcing their fear by recalling the friend's straw house that was blown to bits by heartbreak, or Dad tearing apart Mom's stick "home" twig by twig. The cost of this seclusion is the potential of finding love. Continuing the metaphor, even the most solidly constructed house has doors and windows that can open to let in the light. These chinks (telling friends you're available for coffee with their cute neighbor, going to the poetry reading alone—who knows who you'll meet?) represent a positive step from disconnection to more flexible autonomy, from apprehension to possibility. (The last sentence is meant for the unattached who are reading this book with the hope of finally letting lasting love in the front door.)

Another common motivation for isolating yourself is the fear of merging with a loved one. We all have witnessed friends embark on a passionate love affair and suddenly take a serious, never-before-expressed interest in golf or saltwater aquariums, completely disappearing into the world of "we/us." Perhaps you've even done this yourself. It is natural in the first blush of love to dive into your partner's world as an expression of devotion. In some individuals, though, merging with a loved one can feel like a near-irresistible pull that threatens a complete loss of individual identity. Temptation to fuse together and the fear of doing so are wrapped up in a jumble that makes only one choice feel safe: isolation. If you are unable to build an autonomous boundary to resist this whirlpool, you may choose to withdraw emotionally and physically.

Recognizing this craving helps to avoid being controlled by the urge to merge. Those who were not satisfied in their early years will especially feel this desire. But it is too late for the total blending (as with a mother/infant) to feel gratifying. The key to staying on a steady keel is to aim for an even balance between being an "us" and being a "me," remaining conscious of the fact that, no matter how much we crave it, merging with another is a risky path to adult happiness.

JODI AND DEREK

A good example of the urge to merge—and its pitfalls—is found in Jodi and Derek, a couple whose sexual connection is on the brink of extinction. When the two met in college twelve years ago, this would be the least likely fate either could imagine. Introduced at a football game, their chemistry had enough electricity to light a small town. Thus began a two-year, long-distance relationship complete with all-night phone calls and exhausting train rides made worth it by the passionate lovemaking that highlighted each reunion. The dark side of this all-consuming passion was Jodi's obsession with Derek and—more specifically—with whom he might be spending his time in her absence. She called him each night and panicked if he was not in his room to take the call. Friends worried as she lost ten pounds off her already slim frame. Jodi did not realize that a love so fraught with anxiety was not proof of its truth and depth, but rather a sign of hidden fault lines.

After graduation, Derek and Jodi married and settled into a small apartment in Brooklyn, which somewhat abated her panic that Derek would leave for another woman. As they built their life together, however, her anxiety was replaced by a dread of sleeping with him for fear that she would again become obsessed. On a visceral level, she felt that her identity was at stake.

With time, if Derek initiated, Jodi would agree to intercourse. She knew that sexual intimacy was crucial to making her marriage work. However, her obvious anxiety dampened his pleasure, making Derek feel that he was imposing himself. For Derek to regain his spirited enjoyment of sex with Jodi he must push past his feelings that he was selfishly imposing on her and commit to pursuing a vibrant sex life with his wife. He must tell himself that with patience, Jodi's isolating stance will erode and she will gain comfort in surrendering without losing her autonomy. Jodi will benefit from Derek's reinforcement that it is *her* that he needs and wants. With stubborn persistence, Jodi's fears of disappearing will diminish. Derek's choice to proactively encourage intimacy in his marriage is a form of "good selfish," taking what he needs with the overall knowledge that both will ultimately benefit. (I will discuss the difference between "good selfish" and "bad selfish" in more detail in Chapter 23.)

Extreme autonomy is rigidly self-protective, a behavior that stands in opposition to a lifelong love. Self-sufficiency, on the other hand, gives you the ability to dance to your own music alongside your lover without losing your uniqueness. Bridge-building autonomy is flexible and fluid, providing an important boundary over which you can smile at your partner in appreciation and love.

Chapter 5

SURRENDER VERSUS SUBMISSION
Learning to Yield Without Losing Yourself

During a recent night out in New York, I watched as the spotlight followed two dancers across a small stage, locked in wordless harmony. The steps of the tango gave them the necessary language to negotiate a perfect balance, as each partner's trustworthy arms supported the other's every surrender. Locked in the dance as they were, it was hard to imagine they weren't lovers, just professional dancers perfectly executing this powerful art form. *Perhaps I should send some of my patients off to ballroom-dancing school,* I thought to myself.

The tango has a lot to teach us about how to achieve success in love. Just as in the dance, each partner in a relationship maintains his or her own space, footwork, rhythm, and beat, while moving in sync with the other. Leaning in, they establish the contact necessary to keep the dance alive. In this chapter, you will learn the crucial difference between surrender, which is a conscious choice to give oneself over to the experience of caring, and submission, which is a master/slave power imbalance that threatens the foundation of intimacy.

THE POWER DYNAMICS OF SURRENDER AND SUBMISSION

Many people mistake surrender for submission. The definitions that follow establish a language for understanding the difference and taking more conscious control of your reactions.

Surrender
The conscious choice of openhearted loving.

Submission
An involuntary reaction to feeling overpowered.

Confusing these definitions interferes with connecting with a loved one. If you think that surrender is the same as submission, your natural response to becoming "enslaved" is to hold yourself at a distance.

SURRENDERING

In contemporary gender dynamics, the choice between surrender and submission becomes political. Women—breaking free of time-honored archetypes in which submission was built into their role—have become vigilant to the threat of losing their hard-won power. If surrender is confused with submission, it can seem like an admission of defeat. In actuality, surrender is a *per-*

sonal choice. This deliberate response is supported by a growing number of studies, which, as reported by Patricia Leigh Brown in the *New York Times*, indicate that the best route to *eudaemonia* (the classical Greek term for human flourishing) is giving to and caring about others. Understanding the power of surrender establishes a boundary that holds a belief in your own value in place while reaching out to experience the best in your partner. The decision to surrender to another, as in the tango, supports a balanced and confident life.

SUBMITTING

Alternatively, if you *submit* your self-control to another, your boundaries vanish. An imbalance of power emerges that allows the other to be in charge of you; your free will is trampled. The damage from this "master/slave" scenario can range from a nagging unhappiness born of submerging desires (where to go on vacation, which house to buy, who does the housework) to sleep disorders (you are unable to surrender to sleep because of the anxiety connected to submission), to more nefarious scenes of verbal and physical abuse. A propensity to submit arises when nature and nurture become a perfect storm of fearfulness and timidity. If you grew up shy and with an overbearing parent, you are probably averse to conflict. Now that you are an adult (especially if you are with a person who possesses a strong personality), this tendency makes it even more difficult to say no or stand up for yourself. You become barricaded within, sacrificing an emerged identity and compromising the strength necessary to resist submission.

SUBMISSION AND CONTROL

At its most extreme, submission can occur if one partner intentionally wants to control the other. Explosive anger resulting from the insatiability of such a desire can lead to domestic violence, or at least inequity that is fallout from feeling threatened by the possibility of physical harm. Popular culture shows again and again the frustrated male figure lashing out verbally or physically to control his meeker female counterpart. "One of these days, Alice, POW, right in the kisser!" is Ralph's refrain on *The Honeymooners*. This is meant to make us laugh, but we recognize this same coded threat fifty years later when the doltishly menacing husband of our runaway heroine in 1991's *Thelma and Louise* demands, "Now, you get yer butt back here, Thelma." It is easy to see the environment of negativity that forms if a partner is able to make his spouse submit through the specter of bodily harm. But, how does submission damage relationships within less overt, more peaceable households?

In my practice I often observe couples losing touch with each other over the years, not because one is hitting the other, but because one person feels enslaved over life's details. With work, family, maintaining a house, and paying the bills, a modern, two-income life can be overwhelming. Frequently, one person takes responsibility for the majority of the domestic tasks. In this scenario, the partner (usually the woman) becomes the taskmaster, the nag, the often-unwitting slave master. Conversations tend to begin with "Did you remember to . . ." and "Please don't forget to . . ." and end with "I can't do everything around here!" Over time, the ones submitting to this onslaught of demands become resentful and feel they can never do enough. And, they're right. The taskmaster is chronically disappointed, stirring his or her cauldron of bubbling resentment. Living in a cloud of bitterness rooted in mundane domesticity, it can be difficult to reach a position of equal footing at which surrendering to each other is appealing. The couple in the following story illustrates that believing there is no difference between surrender and submission can risk a long-term partnership.

LANCE AND TOBY

Lance and Toby's marriage was at a standstill when he first met Barbara, his podiatrist. Bubbly, nurturing, and kind-hearted, Barbara seemed to him the opposite of the woman his wife had become: always demanding something of him, usually disappointed, cold in bed.

Lance's amorous adventures (Barbara was not his first affair) were the only areas in his life where he felt he could take the lead. He and Toby both worked at large accounting firms, but she was made partner while he toiled in middle management. At home, his wife doled out tasks like the captain of a foundering ship. She was stern, impatient, and unforgiving of slip-ups. While they used to be able to laugh at his forgetful tendencies—one birthday she presented him with four duplicate sets of keys so he wouldn't panic each time he misplaced them—the joke was now over. Between work and the kids, Toby believed that if she didn't take charge no one would, and the family would fall apart. Her tough outer shell protected a softer vulnerability that Lance saw recede more and more each year.

But for Toby, surrendering to her husband in their partnership was terrifying. When she was growing up, her parents were locked in an endless battle. Toby kept her head down and was largely ignored. She excelled in school and work and hid her soft underbelly. Her view of childhood is that she raised herself. With the inevitable difficulties of adulthood, this conditioned reaction to stress came at a cost: resistance to opening herself up to her lover.

To make matters worse, Lance and Toby's bedroom was awash in uncomfortable silence. Neither would initiate sex. In stark contrast to the way she conducted herself in the office, where she was a leader, in the sexual arena Toby waited for her husband to make the first move. This was rooted in her parents' lack of initiative on her behalf, which she interpreted as undervaluing her. She then internalized this belief about her true value. But Lance, feeling powerless and unable to see through her tough exterior, could not come to bed and suddenly become assertive.

TAKING THE FIRST STEPS TOWARD SURRENDER

Lance's passivity, coupled with Toby's vulnerability in moments such as initiating sex, which was rooted in an early distrust of her parents, drove them further and further apart. Lance acted out his feelings of being pinned down by seeking out women. His affair with Barbara lasted three months, until the day he went for a run, leaving his BlackBerry on the kitchen table. Its beep and shiver caught his nearby wife's attention. Toby then noticed the message and discovered his betrayal. Because she had previously interpreted Lance's resistance to initiation as a low sex drive, the revelation of his affair was devastating for Toby. It reinforced her self-denigrating/self-protective stance. Wanting and not wanting to immediately call it quits, she insisted they go to therapy. Lance resisted the idea: "And I suppose this will be another place where you can tell me what to do, except now you'll have some shrink to back you up!"

"I'm not the one who brought us to this, Lance," she replied. "You got us here. I'm just trying to get us out."

Guilt-ridden and heartbroken, Lance tucked his tail between his legs and followed his wife to couple's therapy sessions. As he better understands himself, Lance now uncomfortably believes he craves merging with another. Submission is the natural response to a yearning to merge: *Maybe if I do exactly what you say and don't make a fuss, I can be close, close, close to you, mommy/girlfriend/wife.* Lance's desire to fuse with his wife, driven by unmet childhood longings, obliterated the ability to experience a natural separation between two adults.

As Toby and Lance unravel their feelings, the cycle of Lance's hunger to submit and Toby's discomfort with surrender is becoming clearer. Closed off and controlling, Toby could not yield to Lance's love in the bedroom or anywhere else. Pining for his elusive wife, Lance became submissive, which resulted in resentment and betrayal.

Both are rediscovering how to be intimate with one another through everyday choices. These decisions can be as simple as Toby, even if she feels tired, initiating sex once a week. Or Lance taking complete charge of some household task, such as managing the bills. These acts open the door to positive change and more closeness in their relationship.

CHOOSE SURRENDER, CHOOSE LOVE

The fundamental challenge of cultivating lasting love is accepting that none of us is perfect. You may be perfect (enough) for one another, but your lover is going to drive you crazy in a myriad of unexpected and maddening ways, and vice versa. Imagine that you and your mate have been going through a rough time. When he suggests the two of you go out for an expensive meal paid for by his selling a restored car at the antique car dealer's convention, you have a choice. Your first reaction may be to reject this peace offering. After all, taking him up on his offer would be "giving in." But refusing to join him, or going along and pouting over your soup, keeps both of you powerless and inhibits the chance for surrendering to the pleasure of the experience. Choosing to be angry enslaves you, and you forgo the opportunity for peace—or at the very least an enjoyable meal.

The other option here is to surrender to the experience. Going to dinner openheartedly is not necessarily a reflection that you forgive your partner's "crimes." Accepting the invitation with no "yes, buts" goes a long way toward building a receptive environment between two people. You could have chosen a punishing power play calculated to elicit some response in him. But rather you opted to take in this little bit of life, and enjoy it. Admittedly, an evening of fine dining may not bring you nearer to a resolution. You could walk away only with the memory of a nice lobster bisque. But, there is a chance it may encourage some openness to listening to each person's point of view.

Certainly the opportunity for reconciliation is greater in this scenario than if you had sat across from him with smoke coming out of your ears. Accept that you feel vulnerable—naked—when you surrender. It definitely won't kill you, and it could make you stronger.

You have the power to create your own happiness specifically by choosing to surrender to love. There are occasions in most of our lives when we feel our well-being is in the hands of another. However, this is almost never actually the case. Whether it is a boss, a parent, child, or a lover, you have the choice to either give them the keys to your peace of mind or take control of it yourself. In the case of a lover, intimacy results when both people surrender to trust and caring for each other, no matter what each moment brings. Intimacy is witnessing the other person's deeper self with no agenda. This means that in the good times and bad, you aim to do life's dance together with synchronized grace while maintaining that vital boundary that prevents you from crumbling into a pattern of submission.

Chapter 6

ESTABLISHING SPACE VERSUS NEGLECT
Balancing Your and Your Partner's
Space Needs

When you are on your first, second, or third date with a new partner, you may joyfully learn that you both love science fiction, grew up as only children, and have physical chemistry that makes you swoon. But chances are, until the relationship develops further, you won't know whether or not you share a need for the same amount of personal space, or—a more likely scenario—whether one of you needs more or less than the other.

A SPACE MISMATCH

Imagine that you come home, eager to snuggle and talk about the day, only to find your partner alone in a darkened room, zoned out in front of a game of computer solitaire. Replies to your conversational openers are exclusively grunts, so, closing the door behind you, you wander down the hall, the bubble of your excitement deflated.

Conversely, maybe *you* are the one reveling in a quiet moment of decompression after a day in which your boss made you cry and December's ugly credit card bill arrived. Just letting your mind focus on the nothingness of the computer game, where there are no stakes and it doesn't matter and no one cares . . . oh, it feels like bliss. Until you hear his keys in the door and your shoulders tense at the thought of someone else's demands at this moment. And you just can't do it. You need to be alone for just a little longer, so you make no effort to communicate, knowing he'll get the message and go away.

Establishing space versus neglect is a unique interpersonal Turning Point in that the individual doing the action and the receiver of the action experience the moment simultaneously. A mismatch occurs when one partner desires abundant alone time and the other has a signature need for togetherness—and feels neglected when his or her loved one pulls away. Is there a way to resolve this relationship hurdle? As you will see, adjusting to another's space requirement offers plenty of opportunities for growth.

SPACE PREDISPOSITIONS

Each person enters an intimate relationship with a built-in comfort level regarding personal space established long before we were verbal. Your concept of space depends on two factors:

1. Biological predisposition
2. Infant/maternal attachment

If you were born introverted (overwhelmed by too much stimulation) and your mother craved attachment, you may have experienced her attentions as intrusive. Or, you may have had a mother that even by an extrovert's standards was invasive, needy, or just plain over the top. In such cases, you would most likely be the person happily playing computer games in the preceding example.

If, however, you wanted contact and your mother was introverted, shy, or distracted by work, her husband, or too many other children, or died when you were young, you may have felt neglected. Now, as an adult, you long for companionship and have little desire to spend time alone. What's more, that same scenario of the distracted mother could have made you into an adult uncomfortable with closeness due to minimal childhood experience with it.

When you're a child, having your space needs match those of your primary caregiver is luck. In adulthood, giving and receiving space without feeling either neglected or smothered is the ideal. Depending on your family histories, you and your partner fall somewhere along the continuum between craving alone time and longing for companionship. Most people are someplace in the middle: needing a breather now and then, but generally happy to enjoy the presence of a loved one. Problems arise, however, when one or both individuals diverge toward the more extreme ends of the spectrum, as in the case of Eduard and Callie.

EDUARD AND CALLIE

A suburban couple, Eduard and Callie both work hard—he as the managing director of a nursing home and she as a stay-at-home mom to two young boys. One evening, they went out to dinner. As Callie perused the wine list, Eduard said, "I wish we had more time like this to ourselves."

Assuming he had complimented her, Eduard was shocked by Callie's viper-rapid response: "I can never give you enough—

enough time, enough sex, enough of me. I'm stretched to the limit, Ed." She paused, taking a deep breath, and softly continued, "And I am happy that today I feel confident enough to tell you this. Ten years ago, I would have swallowed my annoyance."

Eduard spent the rest of the meal—and subsequent days—pensive and worried. He found himself tiptoeing around his wife, as if she were something thin-skinned and slightly dangerous. A few days after their dinner, Eduard came home with an exciting update on a government grant for which the nursing home was a candidate. Feeling confident, he approached Callie after dinner with his good news. "Hold on, let me get the dogs out," she said, corralling the excited animals in the mudroom. Coming back inside, she was on to the next thing, having seemingly forgotten that Eduard had something to tell her. Standing in the kitchen's harsh glow, he watched her scrape the dinner plates into the trash and load the dishwasher, lost in her own world. *I can't believe it; I am married to a complete bitch. She has time for everyone—even the dogs! And apparently I am a notch below the dirty dishes.*

JERRY'S INSIGHT

The distance between them grew, until a chance encounter during a visit from his father, Jerry, led Eduard to question his indictment of Callie as selfish and cruel. Overhearing a phone conversation in the next room, Eduard listened as his dad suggested to his stepmother that he go back to the city, pick up some of her clothes, and drive upstate through the night to be with her and her ill mother. Eduard held his breath during the silence while Jerry listened to her response. Pleadingly, Jerry then said, "But don't you want to sleep with me tonight?" The reply must have been negative, for he soon hung up the phone and flipped on the television.

Eduard's heart hurt for his dad; he wondered how his marriage was faring. Joining him in the den, he innocently asked, "How's Judy doing? Her mom any better?"

"Ah, she's having a hard time of it. I offered to go up, but she said she needs to focus all her energies on her mom. Judy's always been that way, though; independent, won't take the help that's offered."

"I'd get in the car and go up anyway. She needs a shoulder at a time like this."

To Eduard's surprise, Jerry let out a huge guffaw. He swiveled his La-Z-Boy around to face his perplexed son. "I think I'd be headed to divorce court, if I just showed up bags in hand. You can't expect someone who likes their space to be grateful to ya' for invading it. I learned years ago to leave her be when she asks. She always comes back, and I'm happy for it."

Relief began to glow and grow within Eduard. Were he and Callie struggling with a space/distance difference? Was her coldness not, after all, a character flaw? He thought about the similarities in his and his dad's situations: They both seemed to tiptoe around their wives, who needed more space than they did, and both could feel rejected by this difference in his partner.

TOOLS FOR OVERCOMING SPACE ISSUES

There are many possible responses for those who find themselves in Eduard and Callie's situation. Often someone with Callie's space needs, when feeling intruded upon, will choose impenetrable silence. For the receiver, this is akin to being set off on an ice floe. Silence is a powerful nonverbal gesture indicating that you need breathing room, and it gets the point across. So what is wrong with this approach? After all, sometimes silence is the best form of communication. It provides an occasion for self-assessment, increasing your odds of later approaching the other person with clarity. However, isolating a loved one is brutal punishment. Prison systems use it for the worst offenders—solitary confinement.

In most cases, communicating through silence is a barrier-building response to a space mismatch. What do you do, then, if you need quiet to regroup? A boundary-building choice would be to say, for example, "I need to take some alone time. Please offer this to me without assuming it is a rejection of you." If Callie had chosen to explain to Eduard that sometimes she just needs to not be needed, it would give him the opportunity to respond with understanding rather than anger.

She didn't choose that path, however, so what is Eduard to do as the one being cut off? The rejected partner has several options:

1. He can cut Callie off in retaliation, leading to a perpetual cycle of angry silence.
2. He can give her space, accepting that it is impossible to control another person. Doing this, he must manage his reaction to being cut off. Pain connected to loss makes this option challenging.
3. He may engage a third party to speak on his behalf to unravel the meaning of the cutoff.
4. He can make an educated guess concerning Callie's distress. He can then be receptive when she reconnects. Offering curiosity, he may learn why she cut him off (feeling overwhelmed, depressed, the onset of her period or menopause, or just tired of talking and wanting alone time).

It is in Eduard's power to keep the door open. Slamming up against her desire for space will not gain him favor. Ideally, both will inch toward the other. But it is possible that Callie is not going to shift. In the interest of family harmony, it may be up to Eduard to change his perspective. If he is able to not take her need for space personally and learn self-reliance, he can build an approachable boundary around himself that will make their marriage stronger. So, the next time he comes home with news and

Callie seems distracted by the dogs or the dishes, a good strategy would be to hold off on initiating a conversation and instead seek out an activity he enjoys until a more opportune moment for connection arises.

HAPPINESS BOTH TOGETHER AND ALONE

If you feel neglected by a space-craving partner, you might obsessively ruminate about why he is "ignoring" you, not making love to you, spending time with others or alone. This can lead to destructive acting out—tantrums, substance abuse, overspending, sexual misadventures, or moping about hoping for attention.

But there is another option when feelings of loneliness creep in: productive self-reliance. Thomas Dumm, a professor of political science at Amherst College, explores the disparity between being alone and loneliness in his book *Loneliness as a Way of Life*. Dumm states that when we are lonely all others desert us, including our own selves. In loneliness, we are unable to recognize ourselves with the sort of certainty that would allow us to join with others, rather than conform to them. He concludes that loneliness establishes a barrier between the self and the world, leaving the world intact as a torment to the isolated person. On the other hand, a more robust sense of the connections between oneself and others may enable a happier and less lonesome way of being in the world. You move from the position of being on the outside looking in to seeing yourself as part of the group or the couple regardless of what is happening in any moment.

If you love togetherness, you are presented with a clear choice: Learn self-reliance or be miserable. Discovering how to make yourself happy without the aid of others is part of your evolution into a fully functional adult.

On the other hand, if you require much space and alone time, you have a great deal to learn about the joys of sharing. At the outset, it may seem tiring to engage in a conversation rather than the Internet, but moments with a loved one are enriching experiences. Insisting on going solo lessens your chances of being pleasantly surprised by others, and diminishes the possibility of shared happiness.

{ Isolation from yourself leads to despair, while self-reliance leads to pleasurable solitude. Becoming comfortable with the space needed by those you love, whether you like it or not, is a path worth forging. When you successfully negotiate this Turning Point, your connection to others and yourself begins to grow, leading you away from the potential path of loneliness and despair.

Chapter 7

PATIENCE VERSUS PASSIVITY
Maintaining an Enduring Stance

Imagine two people: One is an old, wise man sitting on the side of a mountain, wild-haired or monk bald, depending on your preference. The other, whom we'll call Howard, also sits immobile, but in front of his mother's television set at three in the afternoon. Both men are similarly occupied: sitting in a trancelike state, waiting for something to happen. Which one is exhibiting patience, and which passivity? If you assume, with your limited information, that it is the wise man who is being patient, you are correct; but why?

Many people confuse these two states of being, given that they both imply stillness. Following are the definitions:

Patience is a conscious decision to accept your place in the world, to recognize your limitations as well as the weaknesses of others, and to live in a state of calm readiness.

Passivity manifests itself as an unintentional giving in to the urge to be completely taken care of while being inured to the needs of others. Sleeping too long, consistently being late, making unreasonable demands, and refusing to make difficult choices or take positive action are passive behaviors.

THE REASON HOWARD IS SINGLE

Being passive engenders powerlessness within yourself and with others. In an intimate relationship, passivity affects the couple. It builds barriers and can be especially frustrating when a loved one insists that her immovability is actually a preference for being laid-back. "Hey, relax," the passive person insists. "I'll get to it when I get to it." The irony is that when an individual confuses passivity with being patient, it is difficult for her lover to summon the patience to remain in the relationship. Passivity masked as patience allows people to let themselves off the hook, leaving the "work" (household chores, paying the bills, child care) of building a satisfying adult life solely in another's hands. Resentment develops, constructing barriers that inhibit the chance for a loving, long-term relationship. All too swiftly, the partner of the passive individual becomes the nag, the complainer, the enforcer, resulting in an unhappy power imbalance.

True patience, on the other hand, is a state of being that builds flexible boundaries between people. Instead of creating partnership obstacles, behaving with patience is an active form of acceptance and gratitude. When you are serene, you may notice the imperfections within your partner and yourself, yet you approach these limitations with tolerance. A conscious effort, patience takes self-correction and practice, but over time is an expression of gratitude for your life.

Many types of parenting can lead to passivity. According to Dr. Bonnie Maslin, in her book *Picking Your Battles: Winning Strategies for Raising Well-Behaved Kids*, "A controlling parent saps the will out of a child—they [the children] look passive. A hypercritical parent can paralyze a child—they look passive. A hyperanxious parent frightens a child into paralysis—they look passive." A parent who behaves in such a way as to reduce his child's anxiety may actually prevent a future propensity for passivity.

The criterion for distinguishing between patience and passivity is utilitarian. Does the period of waiting make you feel thankful for the experience (which indicates patience), or does it diminish your sense of control and increase powerlessness (which indicates passivity)? Following is the story of a man who spent fifteen years confusing his passivity for patience, the result of which was a financial reversal for his family.

TIM AND BARBARA

Tim is forty-three years old, handsome, heavyset, and kind, with a soft-spoken, sonorous voice. For the bulk of his professional life, he worked in his family's cosmetics business. Arthur, Tim's father, had a recognizable name in this industry, having been employed by most of the important American cosmetics firms at one time or another.

About fifteen years ago, Arthur decided to manufacture his own cosmetics brand. Tim was in charge of marketing these products across the United States, with housewives selling the cosmetics, similar to Avon. Since Tim was out in the field with the sellers and buyers, he soon discovered the flaws in the way their business was structured. However, Arthur was enamored with the firm's main chemist/designer—Clarice LeBon—as evidenced by the fact that he named the company after her. Clarice, a Frenchwoman who appeared a decade younger than her actual age, had captured the imagination of her widowed boss, Arthur—and she knew it. A rivalry soon emerged between Tim and Clarice. Whenever Tim suggested improvements, Clarice would privately say to Arthur, "Don't fix what isn't broken."

Over the next ten years, as their originally exciting business became increasingly unprofitable, Tim tried to lobby his father and even his brother, Troy, the business comptroller, to consider his innovative ideas. Arthur received these proposals, complimented Tim on the most creative, doable thoughts, but the final say belonged to Clarice. Coming home to his wife, Barbara, who was one of the company's stalwart saleswomen, Tim would bemoan his ineffectual dealings with his father.

"He's infatuated with her! He's an old man, for heaven's sake, and she flirts her way all the way to the bank."

Looking up from one of her many knitting projects, Barbara calmly listened to his customary refrain. It was like a familiar song on the radio; she had only to hear the opening chords to know where it was headed. Years ago, she used to respond by encouraging Tim to look for another job rather than fight this losing battle with his dad. He would agree to "keep an ear to the ground," but nothing changed. Most nights, having vented his frustration, he would go out to the garage to enjoy his nightly ritual of getting mildly stoned and noodling around on his guitar. Their two children had their own lives, so Barbara was left alone in the quiet house. She made enough scarves and mittens to warm an army.

THINGS FALL APART

Recently, just before an economic downturn, "Clarice LeBon" was sold at a fire sale to its largest competitor, basically for the customer list. The buyer didn't even want the equipment, and of course it retained very few of Tim's carefully honed sales force. Now a salesman for an exercise equipment company, and beginning to take some steps forward, Tim has come to accept that his marijuana-fueled evenings, combined with his overattachment to his father and the family business, fed into his passivity and fear of going out on his own. By telling himself that he was being "patient" with his father's intransigence, he squandered two decades of his professional life's creativity, self-progress, and financial security. Tim berates himself for putting his family—including two college-age children—in this position.

And, what of Barbara? Does she join Tim in his flagellation, wishing she'd pushed him harder? Does she show her displeasure at their dwindling life savings by punishing him with silent disapproval? Actually, Barbara says nothing, no "I told you so," no withholding of sex. She has made a conscious decision to move on with her life, taking back her old job at a pediatric dentist's office to earn some money. Barbara isn't perfect either. But she is a happy woman enjoying what she sees as her good fortune: a job, a husband, children—a full life. Her patience and support eventually helped give Tim the inclination to be kind to himself, and to join a twelve-step program for marijuana users. Now they spend their evenings together, four hands keeping busy plucking strings and weaving yarn.

ARE YOU PASSIVE OR PATIENT?

The Turning Point of passivity versus patience can be confusing, and may have a dramatic effect on your life and the happiness of your partner. A tendency toward passivity can be diagnosed through the following questions.

1. Do you avoid change at all costs?
2. Do you overeat, drink, or take any mind-altering substance?
3. Do you sleep more than you need to, in the car, your office, in your brown chair?
4. Do you notice that tasks pile up at home or at work?
5. Do you find that the more these tasks pile up, the less you feel like tackling them?

6. Did you hope for more out of life than you are getting?

7. Are you overly grateful for a flirtatious encounter?

8. Do you hold back on saying something unpleasant, almost to the last minute—the "door-knob theory"—saying or doing what is difficult only as you are leaving the room?

9. Do you often want out, escape, relief from what is occurring?

10. Do you love a high—gambling, illicit sex, racing to catch a plane, and so on?

Give yourself 1 point for each affirmative answer. A score of 10 is pure passivity, which is likely to have a diminishing effect on a long-term relationship. If your score is in the midrange, you could have some passivity that may or may not interfere with your happiness. Keep a close eye on how strictly you hold yourself accountable in your life.

Now take the patience quiz. The higher your score, the more patience you have, which empowers both you and your loved one.

1. You are rarely irritable.

2. You keep yourself occupied when waiting.

3. You are grateful for small things in your life.

4. You do not feel entitled to anything in particular.

5. Your friends may have more things, kids, family, money—whatever you value. This does not build resentment in you.

6. You are a good sport in defeat.

7. When someone you love disappoints you, you can let it go and go on with your life.

8. You can sit for a long period of time and read, meditate, practice yoga, and so on.

9. You rarely raise your voice in anger.

10. You feel the love around you and you return it.

It is possible to have a low passivity score and a low score on patience. This could indicate that you are more aggressive than you realize and that you could be crowding or offending people completely unintentionally. (See the following chapter, Benign Boundaries versus Emotional Tyranny, for an in-depth discussion on that Turning Point.)

> Passivity is a wolf in sheep's clothing: It can mimic patience and provide fleeting moments of satisfaction. Over time, however, passivity destroys intimacy and dismantles trust because it overburdens your partner to shoulder the bulk of the responsibility of your shared life. The better choice is patience: an active state of being that opens up a space between two people, allowing for missteps along the way. Given the fact that none of us is faultless, being patient is a crucial ingredient for maintaining a lifelong love.

Chapter 8

BENIGN BOUNDARIES VERSUS EMOTIONAL TYRANNY
Establishing Borders That Build Connections

Maybe you are vegan; you never work on the Sabbath; you are a dog person, or a cat person; you floss twice a day or not at all. Regardless, you are understandably attached to what you believe to be the right way to live. In a relationship, however, blind insistence on being right can lead to trouble. Taking critical judgment to the extreme, emotional tyrants believe they are correct to the point of demanding conversion from their partners. Furthering a climate of potential conflict, they refuse to meet halfway. "Never," "absolutely not," and "because that's the way it is," are some key phrases the tyrant uses to impose his or her will.

THE BRITTLE NATURE OF TYRANNY

The choice of emotional tyranny is one of blind action. Instead of listening, this dictator lectures, screams, and preaches. He will also enforce his position by "punishing" the unwavering partner through lack of cooperation or a refusal to hear a different point of view. By not taking into account the other person's position, the emotional bully denies the relationship a chance for a fully cooperative partnership.

When you act with emotional tyranny, you—usually without conscious awareness—hope that an onslaught of words and a refusal to bend will eventually wear down your partner. The folly of this wish lies in your secret dream that one day your loved one will approach you, saying, "Now I get it! Thank you so much for teaching me what is of course, without a doubt, the right thing to do. What could I have been thinking?" This unlikely scenario is most often the opposite of what actually results from emotional tyranny: distance, anger, and the breakdown of communication.

What is the other choice to be made when one person's right is their loved one's wrong? Is there reconciliation without complete agreement? Yes. Because your ability to implement elastic, benign boundaries during a dispute gives you the necessary distance to cut short your urge to become tyrannical. By implementing benign boundaries you increase your chance of achieving the connection you seek with your partners. Saying "I believe we should turn right but I am willing to go on for several blocks your way to find out if I am mistaken" rather than "Turn right! You always take the wrong road" is a concrete example of using benign boundaries. Remember, *barriers* impede communication and clear *boundaries* encourage it. When you can see the world through the experience of your partner, you gain empathy, which fosters comfort. Rather than standing on the outlying shore "on principle," you are building a bridge to the other person. Refusing to engage in emotional tyranny is, for those who are susceptible to bullying, a conscious effort to stay flexible and psychologically supple. Just as a healthy tree bends in the wind, flexibility prevents you from becoming brittle.

JOAN AND RICHARD

Joan, a plastic surgeon, and Richard, a design-oriented architect, spent years of their marriage navigating this issue. Although a devoted husband and clearly in love with his wife, Richard had a tendency to be unpredictable and unreliable. For Joan, these qualities at first highlighted his artistic bent, to which her type-A, business-minded personality was attracted. Joan, unlike some of her girlfriends who had been married for only three or four years, was rarely bored with her husband.

As they approached their forties, life got more complicated in a hurry. Both were at a level in their careers at which constant work was non-negotiable. To add to the pressure, Joan knew that if they were going to have kids, now was the time. After one year of trying to get pregnant and another difficult year of fertility treatments, she was pregnant with twins.

The kids did nothing to cure Richard's fly-by-the-seat-of-his-pants disposition, which Joan had so admired in her thirties. He was terribly unsuited to all the details that went into child care. Bottle temperatures and nursery school hours, cash for the babysitter, doctor appointments: It all went against his nature. "Too bad," Joan said to his protests. "I need some help here. I work too. How can I rely on you when you can't do this one simple thing?" A few years later: "Do you know how embarrassing it was to get a call from the school that you forgot to pick up Henry and William?" And, finally: "The bank called. Did you ACTUALLY forget to pay the mortgage?" Richard tried, but was focused on his passion projects at work. The more Joan complained, the more time he spent at the office. Joan's incessant criticism was an understandable reaction to a frustrating situation, but she was *reacting* rather than choosing how to *respond*.

To an outside observer, it was clear that she had become an emotional tyrant.

During the twins' earliest years, Joan and Richard barely spoke unless it was in recriminations (her) and excuses (him). Their sex life deteriorated from once a month to special occasions, and then to almost never. Richard's reaction to unremittingly feeling criticized was to retreat emotionally and physically. This eventually led him to late nights spent in front of the computer, surfing the web, looking at pornography. Ironically, his sessions at the computer left him feeling even more down than did his interchanges with Joan.

RICHARD BREAKS FREE

The breaking point arrived the day Joan became curious about what kept Richard at the computer until late in the evening. Looking up the browser history confirmed her worst suspicions. She was tyrannical before, and her anger now reached new heights.

But Richard had had enough and, in a way, was relieved to end his secret. His actions were a result of his own sadness, and he realized that he needed to shift some things within himself. He heard Joan's anger and let her yell, but instead of slinking off to lick his wounds, he accepted her fury and resolved to look within for the strength to be a better, happier husband.

In time, Richard made good use of therapy and a class in religion and he started to resist allowing Joan's recriminations to negatively affect him. Richard's ability to put a personal boundary in place created a new atmosphere in their home. He was discovering how to rely first and foremost on himself for his happiness. He began to hold steady against Joan's barbed criticisms and create his own criteria of what was acceptable. She subliminally sensed his new boundary and reflexively began to respect him for it. And, thanks to his newly found confidence, Richard had the energy and will to become more reliable. Joan gradually spent less time pointing out his faults and, noticing Richard changing, saw the positive results of being a more peaceful presence in his life.

DEVELOPING EMOTIONAL INTELLIGENCE

Joan and Richard, perhaps sensing a breaking point of their marriage, did something that in the end saved it: They began to think about the impact their reactive behavior was having. Dr. Daniel Goleman, in his seminal work, *Emotional Intelligence*, determined that emotional competencies such as self-awareness and empathy are even more important than intellect in establishing a person's success. Emotional intelligence, or EQ, can come to the rescue of any relationship sinking in tyrannical barriers. A tyrant such as Joan needed to develop the EQ to empathize with Richard's experience without obliterating her reality. In so doing she broke the cycle of her aggressive behavior.

Blame, recriminations, and abundant criticism—the tactics of the emotional tyrant—will never succeed in changing a loved one. Why would they? Like an alchemist attempting to squeeze gold from a pile of rocks, the tyrant wastes her energy on a futile effort to force a connection (according to her own vision of it, of course). The result can be an impermeable fortress of barriers that impede the growth of the couple.

ARE YOU A TYRANT?

How can an "energetic" person become aware that she is, in fact, a tyrant? Look closely at both your partner's behavior and your own. Are you repeating the same phrase over and over again like a battering ram, attempting to break down the castle walls of your lover's will? Is your partner merely compliant, going about his chores but not offering affection or good cheer? If the answer to both questions is yes, there is a serious problem to address. If a despot is able to batter her partner into what she wants him to do, she may inadvertently trigger depression and despair in someone she has committed to loving and supporting.

CREATING A TYRANT

Many of the barriers you set up can be traced back to childhood. It is not surprising to discover that dictatorial tendencies are rooted, for example, in having grown up in a large family where many siblings clamored for attention. Such a person may be conditioned to yell, scream, claw, and kick in order to get any attention, including love. A fear of invisibility reinforces the adaptive defense of developing a dominant will and an ability to dig in your heels to get what's desired.

Joan and Richard's struggle is a reflection of their individual childhood dramas, which continue to play out in their adult lives. Joan's girlhood left a mark of fearfulness. Her mother was depressed but unwilling to seek treatment. She frequently threatened suicide, leaving Joan regularly feeling on the verge of abandonment. Flash-forward thirty years, and it's a short leap to see how Richard's unreliability triggers Joan's worst fear. Her choice of emotional domination is a clear defensive stance. Every disparagement, every criticism she has of Richard is the little girl inside of Joan screaming, "Please don't leave me!" The irony is that Joan's aggression only increases the likelihood of her fear being realized.

Joan's father did nothing to decrease her oppressive tendencies. A bully in the truest sense, his steady criticism of his daughter left an indelible mark. It also reinforced the learned notion that tyrannical behavior was normal and acceptable. Her child's mind understood why he berated her. Joan had the double flaw of being a girl and the next in line after her mother gave birth to a stillborn baby boy. She felt like a "replacement" child who could never measure up to the one her parents lost.

Richard, on the other hand, grew up in a family that was repressed but stable. His parents were deeply religious and unaccustomed to the demonstrative emotion that he craved. Everything was muffled in a vague politeness. As he grew, Richard saw less value in stability and longed for physical affection and unconditional acceptance. At first, he found that in Joan. When their lives became more complicated and he was faced with Joan's anger, he acted out just as he would have as a teenager. *She can't control me,* he thought, as he slunk off to his computer and "rebelled" by watching pornography.

TAKING CHILDHOOD NEEDS INTO ADULTHOOD

Unfulfilled needs and desires originating from your childhood family live on within you. These shadow children (a childhood self that remains a part of you, even now that you are grown) can, if you are not diligent, affect your relationships by building unnecessary fear-based barriers. Recognizing this, you can make the intentional decision to revisit the past and to become aware of when you are repeating it. You can then encourage your mature, adult self to create the flexible boundaries necessary to positively alter your fate. It follows that happiness flows from the feeling of true, vibrant, hard-won human connections that we all crave. In the case of emotional tyranny, the chance of a couple achieving lifelong, fulfilling togetherness is slim as long as the tyrant stomps on his or her partner's limits and instead establishes an emotional dictatorship. The chance for true connection is lost.

Joan and Richard are now thriving. A breakthrough came when Richard fought hard to convince Joan that moving into a new apartment—one that he designed—was the right choice. At first she didn't even consider it, and, falling back on old habits, dug in her heels, remembering Richard's past unreliability. Joan pictured herself dealing with the hassle of moving while Richard was out having fun and leaving the real work to her. But he held his ground. He no longer needed to look to her for approval; he now gave that to himself. Joan sensed his determination and took a risk. She acquiesced, and Richard, now comfortable and confident, proved himself by staying by her side through the renovations and decorating decisions. After much hard work on both their parts, Joan and Richard had vanquished tyranny.

At every age over the course of a lifetime, you are faced with new and different challenges. Becoming an emotional tyrant is a common reaction to these challenges, especially from your twenties through middle age. Insisting you are right and not entertaining the possibility that another person's point of view is valid is a shot to the heart of a satisfying, long-term partnership. Emotional tyranny throws up barriers (brick walls) and simultaneously tramples boundaries (more like a picket fence). It is only through the recognition of tyranny and subsequent efforts to establish restrictions on our own "over the top" expressiveness that the cycle can be broken.

Chapter 9

AWARENESS OF LIMITS VERSUS EMOTIONAL RECKLESSNESS
Embracing the Power of Self-Control

Emotional recklessness is an impulse-driven behavior that disregards boundaries. A virtual stampede of emotions, it can both attract and repel loved ones, but over time may push them away. You know your limits have been breached when, looking back on an encounter, you feel discomfort or irritation. In a social setting, emotional recklessness is easy to spot: Who hasn't been backed into a corner at a cocktail party listening to a virtual stranger's intimate health problems or ugly divorce proceedings? Your eyes scan the room, sending desperate SOS signals. The anxiety you feel is the result of the limits of your comfort zone being violated.

That conversational terrorist you meet at a social gathering is unaware of the boundaries of others. Internally driven, this person has a tendency toward thoughtlessness, wearing blinders when it comes to other people's tolerance levels. This emotionally reckless person can alienate loved ones and strangers alike by being insensitive to how his or her behavior, such as aggressively seeking intimacy, or being highly critical or overbearing, is received. But losing friends and lovers is not the only price to be paid. Chronically giving in to immediate urges can have a destructive effect on one's equilibrium, providing little room for quiet moments of introspection that allow us to gain self-knowledge and wisdom.

SALLY AND ALEHANDRO

From an early age, Sally was taught the opposite of quiet introspection. She adored her father, Lou, and he lapped it up. The two had an extraordinary bond and enjoyed each other's company tremendously. Witty and exuberant, they were a virtual comedy duo entertaining Sally's quiet mother and less dynamic, bookish brothers. No one could compete with the "Sally/Daddy Show." Often, Lou would come home late from a business trip and get her up out of bed, even on school nights. "Up and at 'em, sunshine! No rest for the weary!" Dragging herself down the stairs, fifteen-year-old Sally would muster up the energy to transform an average school day into a story that would amuse. Teachers became comic-book villains, and she the scrappy heroine outwitting them all. "That's my girl!" Lou would exclaim, guffawing over his nightcap.

Sally eventually became a development executive always on the hunt for the next hot film project. She was a road warrior. For the strangers she encountered on planes and in airport lounges, she continued her lifelong tradition of entertaining, expending an astonishing amount of energy during each interaction. Sally was unaware she could choose to enjoy privacy or *not* share herself when traveling. Her emotional recklessness prevented her from making this distinction; she felt compelled to go for the laugh each time, rather than become aware of her own and others' limits.

For her partner, Alehandro, Sally can at times be the most entertaining, exciting person he has ever encountered, or exceedingly tiring. They met when Sally went on vacation to his native Lisbon, Portugal. Alehandro, a wine rep half her age, was not unaccustomed to receiving attention from female tourists, but Sally pursued him with unusual gusto after they danced at a club one night. Not knowing how to find him again, she called his office pretending to be someone from the U.S. Embassy, and learned his address. When she appeared at his apartment unannounced, Alehandro was flattered, if a bit put off by her pursuit. After all, in his culture, women tended to leave the big gestures to the men. However, that night began an intense romance that eventually led him to ask for a transfer to follow her to New York, where his company had a distributorship.

SALLY CALMS THE DIVA WITHIN

Months later, fighting bitterly nearly every day, Alehandro felt that Sally could not be still and consistently overstepped his boundaries. She had recently thrown a late-night party at their apartment without consulting him, and he had been so angry he locked himself in their bedroom in protest. Sally felt that until he would contribute to the household finances, make plans independently of her, and curb his screaming and pickiness, she would fight for her right to live her life as she wished.

Her greatest gift—her ability to meet anyone, anytime, anywhere—had created a barrier in her relationship. She shares herself so easily that Alehandro feels it cheapens their bond. It has also created an obstacle to self-knowledge, a barrier to living the creative, productive life she is more than capable of achieving. Sally's downtime, when she is quiet, not performing, and looking like she is doing nothing, is almost nonexistent. Conditioned to be emotionally reckless by her boundary-stomping father, Sally has never learned to be comfortable in a calm setting. After all, who is she, what is she worth, without an audience?

Sally's openness to adventure is working to her advantage now that she is in therapy. Becoming comfortable with the idea of boundaries is helping her establish a more reliable presence in her business life. She is also beginning to listen with more seriousness to Alehandro's complaints, and, as Sally settles into this new stage of maturity, their bond is growing stronger.

VARIATIONS OF EMOTIONAL RECKLESSNESS

In an intimate relationship, it takes time to realize whether either person is being emotionally reckless. Open to connection at first blush, you may welcome or even initiate the middle-of-the-night phone calls and twenty-four-hour dates. Ah, the romance of flying across the country just to enjoy dinner with your lover! These are the stories you imagine someday telling your grandkids. But what may seem romantic now could cause disruptions down the road if behavior once enjoyed as spontaneous presently encroaches on the limits of your partner. For example, you may cherish taking showers with your lover each morning. If she instead likes her quiet time to bathe and prepare for the day, can you respect her restrictions, or do you complain that she's shutting you out? As reiterated throughout this book, recognizing and respecting each other's boundaries is a key component to keeping love alive. Recklessness, while it may accelerate intimacy by boldly peeling back our outer layers, can threaten long-term happiness.

In order to determine whether you are reckless or merely spontaneous and honest, notice if your way of being leads others to barricade themselves against you or move closer to you because they know where you stand. Showing others what you are thinking and feeling can be a helpful expression of personal boundaries because you are not asking the other person to be a mind reader. It also respects the other person's capacity to be responsive. On the other hand, overwhelming others with your emotionality, personality, or actions is a barrier-building stance—often done inadvertently. A way to recognize and counteract this tendency is by becoming aware of a loved one's limits. You become attentive to another person's limits in one of two ways:

1. If he or she speaks, make sure you listen.
2. Otherwise, tune in to social cues, such as body language and tone. Social illiteracy can be emotionally and financially expensive: Social illiterates often only know they overstepped the other person's boundaries when the partner asks for a divorce.

SANDRA AND CLARENCE

As in Sally's example, often a reckless person has experienced a childhood in which boundaries were violated emotionally, physically, or both. Sandra and Clarence, parents of two-year-old Scott, are at risk for continuing the careless legacy begun by their respective caregivers. Sandra grew up in a large household in Singapore with her father and nine half siblings. Her beautiful opera-singer mother took wing when Sandra was four years old, leaving her to be abused, criticized, and made to sleep in the attic, Cinderella-style. Clarence feels a connection to Sandra because he too suffered in childhood. His stepfather beat him and his brothers for the slightest infraction and called them stupid, blockheads, and worthless idiots. He spent the first fifteen years of his life dreaming of escape.

Clarence left his first wife, claiming she was too critical. Frequently he feels that same itch to run when Sandra harangues him about anything from his shirt-and-tie combination to his parenting skills. Sandra, beautiful as well as successful as a derivatives trader with an international bank, absorbed the skill of eviscerating another from her childhood tormentors and frequently turns her sharp wrath on her husband. To her mind, she's "cutting through the bullshit," but for Clarence, his wife is repeating in him that familiar feeling of being crushed by another person. His boundaries breached, he shuts down, and dreams of divorce.

HARSH WORDS, DIFFICULT REALIZATIONS

Last year, in the car coming home from a friend's holiday party, their young son slept peacefully in his car seat in the back. Up front, however, peace was nowhere in sight. Sandra's sharp features took on a devilish quality in the intermittent light of the oncoming cars. She broke the tense silence with: "You know, I think June and Harvey had a more enlightened conversation with our damn toddler than with you."

"I'm not going to perform for your friends like a monkey," Clarence replied. "The fact that we have nothing in common is no comment on my conversational skills."

"Then you must have nothing in common with most people, because I don't ever see anyone wowed by your sparkling personality. I wonder, do they have adult education courses in charm?"

Their voices rose as they made their way through the tree-lined neighborhoods toward home. Looking in the rearview mirror, Clarence suddenly cut her off, whispering, "Shit." Catching his meaning, Sandra turned around to meet her son's gaze. "It's okay, baby, Daddy and I are just up here chatting." Ashamed, both were silent for the rest of the ride, making private vows to change a pattern of conflict that threatened to affect Scott's peace of mind.

Presently, this couple understands why they are drawn to each other, as well as the pitfalls of their togetherness. Clarence is working on being less reactive to Sandra's emotional recklessness, and Sandra is becoming aware of how her harsh feedback affects her husband and others. They wish to stay together, yet both are haunted by unfinished hurts replayed in their union. Scott is the beneficiary of these two histories colliding. Now, they have a choice: to repeat childhood pain, or to invent a manner of living in the present in which their own and other people's limits are taken into consideration, including their beloved son's.

OVERCOMING EMOTIONAL RECKLESSNESS

One strategy for conquering emotional recklessness is what I call "getting across the street"; in other words, detaching (Chapter 13 develops the difference between detaching and withdrawing in greater detail). In intimate relationships especially, it can be difficult to see a situation or conflict clearly. Like looking at a painting up close, you see the brush strokes and texture but not the whole image. By actively separating yourself from your loved one, which can be done by taking one, two, or more deep breaths when you notice you are tense, you may discover new answers emerging and find that the temptation to trample boundaries is lessening.

As I did with Sandra, I sometimes advise my patients to pretend for a moment that their partner is their client—someone you don't want to anger, and with whom you may need to accomplish some forward movement. How would you treat such a person? With respect, politeness? Simple courtesy can—and often does—allow the breathing room that is necessary for controlling excessive emotionality. In this role, when you are more centered, you can teach yourself how to behave in a relationship in which you have intense investment and a tendency to lose your center.

{ In becoming aware of your own and your partner's limits—and actively deciding not to breach them—your gain is twofold. First, your interactions tend toward harmony and longevity. Second, you acquire the self-knowledge to negotiate life and relationships with the hard-won wisdom of adulthood.

Chapter 10

EMBRACING CHANGE VERSUS PRESERVING THE STATUS QUO
Being Flexible in the Face of Change

If you look over your shoulder at the life you have lived so far, you will see that there are certain moments that stand out from the rest. Should you have stayed in Seattle, broken up with the guy, married the other guy, taken that job abroad? Would you have been happier, more stimulated, terrified, miserable? All of these choices represent the decision to either embrace change or maintain the status quo. You may take a leap of faith into the unknown happily and with positive results, while another may look over that cliff and back slowly away, to an equally pleasant end. Where do you stand? There is a personal formula for tolerance of change that you should decipher.

CHANGE COMPATIBILITY

Of course, being receptive to change or staying with the tried and true becomes a more complicated equation when you introduce a loved one into the mix. If your partner floats from job to job and is eager to change apartments year after year, you had better be on board for a lifetime of variety. And perhaps you are.

Change can become a negative force, however, if you are not as eager as your lover for frequent life adjustments. Staying in one place, embracing the slow build, may give you security and comfort. Maintaining the status quo is grounding and can keep fear at bay, at least for a while. If this strategy does not appeal to your partner, conflict is inevitable and especially frustrating if what originally attracted you to each other was his sense of adventure balanced by your steady, secure love. Decisions such as when or if to have children and how to spend or save your money can be made more challenging by a mismatched tolerance of change.

With patience and a flexible give-and-take, partners who fall on opposing sides of this Turning Point can still find contentment. However, an extreme desire for either variety or sameness can be barrier-building and impede long-term love. If a yearning for change is reactive—a product of avoidance, recklessness at the expense of others, or a cover-up for the panic of growing older—it can cause chaos. We see this phenomenon when couples enter their forties and are faced with the combination of young children at home, careers they feel burdened by, and the inevitable slide toward middle age. The crisis that ensues is familiar and recognizable: affairs, overspending, heightened disagreements, and divorce. The couple in the following story fit the definition of how a conflicting hunger for change can lead to stress.

ALICIA AND BRETT

Alicia's girlfriends were jealous. She was living the dream: a good man who worked hard; three young, happy children; and enough money so that she could stay at home and still hire a cleaning service once a week. It was modestly wonderful. So why did Alicia feel itchy, restless, in need of an excitement that would shake up the numbing predictability of her life? In bed one night after lovemaking, Alicia proposed to Brett that they go downtown that weekend and check out a swingers club she had heard about. Hesitant at first, Brett eventually agreed, fearing that he would seem like less of a man if he refused. After all, what husband would complain that his wife was *too* sexually adventurous?

Fast-forward three years: Alicia and Brett are still involved in their local swingers scene. While it was fun at first, eventually it created confusion in their feelings toward each other, especially Alicia's toward Brett. A moving target, her desire for excitement continued, making her wonder whether she and Brett were a good match. Her eyes wandered to other men—and women—who were less conservative. As well, the children were getting older and catching a whiff of their parent's unconventional lifestyle. This created confusion, especially for Steven, their ten-year-old first-born son.

Sensing her dissatisfaction, but not understanding it, Brett became openly critical of his wife. His frustration soared as the kids went wild—pushing their mother to seek out her limits and finding none there. He was forever coming home to find her on the phone with, in his words, "God knows who." Feeling under siege, Alicia's first instinct was to look for an escape. She encountered a man at her gym and began meeting him for coffee. Although a physical affair had not yet begun, she felt, with excitement tempered by trepidation, that something would happen soon. Alicia was now living the prediction of the English poet Philip Larkin when he wrote, "Life is first boredom/Then fear." She had reacted to her boredom with action, but was now living with the consequences. Her concern over destroying her family was growing ominously.

Consciously acknowledging her feelings of suffocation and entrapment was a positive first step. That summer, she and Brett took separate vacations for time to think. She returned home from her trip to Key West with her girlfriends with an idea: She loved to travel, and would become a travel agent, specializing in group travel for established organizations. This would serve two functions: It would get her out of the house during the day, and it would provide the family with extra money and incentive to take trips together. Brett was thrilled. His wife seemed to have found an outlet for her restlessness. And she had. Yet, Alicia still felt she had to be vigilant against her impulse to push the envelope. She changed gyms to avoid seeing her coffee "friend" but still caught men's eyes on the street and wondered, "What if ?"

Being excessively attracted to change can put happiness with a loved one at risk. On the other hand, clinging to the way your life has always been can also be disruptive to peace of mind because transformations inevitably occur, whether you cause them to happen or not. Resisting variation, and then being surprised by forces beyond your control, triggers anger, despair, and feelings of helplessness. That's just what happened to Kenneth, whose story follows.

CARLA AND KENNETH

When Kenneth first met Carla at a friend's party in Chicago, he was immediately attracted to her easy laugh and her long legs. Later that month, on their second date, he became even more smitten when she mentioned she didn't want children. Kenneth had dreamed up a vision for what his adult life would look like: a sleek apartment in the city, a prestigious position at the University of Chicago, and a beautiful wife who would help him entertain their friends and accompany him to the city's many jazz clubs. Diapers were nowhere in the mix.

Five years later, Kenneth and Carla were married and loving their urban lifestyle. There was one catch: Carla, now thirty-five years old, had decided she wanted a child after all. So, after a year of cajoling, bargaining, and a bit of trickery, Carla was pregnant and blissful. Kenneth watched warily as his wife's formerly svelte body swelled and changed. When the baby was born—a beautiful boy—he remained absent emotionally, while Carla became engrossed by her duties as a new mom.

Slowly, a workable pattern ensued, and Kenneth felt he was adjusting admirably to their new lifestyle. Order was preserved until the inevitable occurred. Life up and handed the couple another momentous change: Carla's beloved father passed away, leaving her an inheritance. Stricken with grief, but holding it together, Carla dreaded telling her husband her dad's proviso—that they move out of the city and use the money to buy a "proper home" for his grandson. She knew Kenneth had grown up in the suburbs and vowed never to go back.

"This feels an awful lot like blackmail from the beyond," Kenneth said. "We wouldn't know anyone out there; we'd be eating at Applebee's every night!"

"I swear, if it's terrible, we can come back to the city. But it will be good for us. You'll see—more space, better schools . . . trees!"

Reluctantly, Kenneth agreed to use her father's money to buy a four-bedroom ranch house forty-five minutes outside of the city. Very quickly, he began to feel his commute was unbearable. While Carla enjoyed the neighborhood and joined a book club, Kenneth spent more and more nights in the city with friends. When he did come home in the evening, he slept in the guest room; she didn't follow.

BRIDGING THE GAP

The chasm that developed between Carla and Kenneth was due to a fundamental imbalance: her ability to accept change coupled with his need to keep the status quo. Within the hothouse of their marriage, this distinction was difficult to see. From Carla's perspective, Kenneth "never put out an effort," while Carla "was a spoiled brat," according to her husband. How could they build a bridge back to one another?

The way back in would be to meet in the middle. Carla lacked empathy for Kenneth's plight, refusing to tease him out of his bad mood when he got home and using the baby as an excuse to avoid sex. If she could reach out, perhaps he would accept that living in the suburbs for a few years was worth it to keep his family intact. For his part, Kenneth had become inflexible. Although he had agreed to take his father-in-law's money, he never did the internal work of letting go of his distaste for the suburbs, based on lingering teenage emotions. Refusing to see any positive elements in their new lives, he could only focus on perceived losses. His commitment to this negativity built a barrier between him and his wife.

LIFE CYCLE EVENTS

It is often the case that an intimate relationship will move along swimmingly until faced with what are called life cycle events—births, communions, bar mitzvahs, moving, weddings, empty nests, or death. On these transitional occasions, people's tolerance of change—or lack thereof—becomes obvious. When, like Kenneth and Carla, you discover that a loved one is unable to happily handle a grand shift, patience and flexibility are the keys to navigating the unexpectedly rough waters.

Unavoidable life cycle events can throw you into a whirlwind of fear and destructive behavior when clinging to the way it always has been seems essential for preserving equilibrium.

One life cycle event that can especially reveal distress due to change is the death of a family member. Emotions run high, and anger often erupts over perceived slights at funerals and wakes, anger that seems disproportionate to the "crime." Looking beyond the obvious, there could be resentment at the deceased for leaving—a logical but often unacceptable thought. These sad events also cause us to pause and reflect on our own mortality—the ultimate reminder of our inability to control the forces of change.

ACQUIRING THE WISDOM TO HANDLE CHANGE

Because life is sure to present you with unknowable surprises and unforeseen challenges, learning to accept—and even initiate—

change can give you a sense of control, a happy alternative to helpless stagnation. When you are face-to-face with an important challenge, what changes do you need to make, even if disrupting your comfort zone distresses you? Knowing what changes to instigate requires meditative time spent getting to know yourself, so that when you make them, they represent your best self.

Similarly, if you're obsessed with variety, you could find yourself adrift, never having opted to stay in school, with a partner, in a city or profession. While exciting, this lifestyle can cause wear and tear on most long-term relationships. If you relish the thought of being a lone adventurer, you are on the right path. But if you also crave intimacy, you should approach your need for change with thoughtful accountability. If you find yourself about to engage in spontaneous behavior that seems too good to pass up, ask yourself questions such as these: "Would this act make my relationship stronger?" "Will I be tempted to lie about this?" "Am I initiating this change to avoid feeling depressed, sad, despairing, or is this something that will authentically improve my job/life/happiness?"

"Change is the only constant." This bit of wisdom remains as valid today as when the ancient Greek philosopher Heraclitus first spoke it. Indeed, as he poetically put it: "We can never step into the same stream twice." As with each Turning Point in this book, you stand a better chance of keeping love alive by taking a moment to look behind the curtain, in this case at how your attitudes toward change dictate your behaviors. In that moment, that thoughtful pause, you can distinguish between what will build a bridge to a loved one and what will tear it down.

Part II
Communication

Chapter 11

TAKING RESPONSIBILITY VERSUS BLAME
Owning Your Part of the Problem

Powerful and insidious, blame lies in wait, its crooked finger itching to point out fault. It self-righteously takes the heat off of you during an argument. It stews with grim satisfaction when your partner comes home late yet again. And, my, what a long memory it has! The passage of time is meaningless when it comes to the power of laying blame on a loved one. We may forget what time to pick up the kids, but we can be elephants when it comes to ancient resentments. Old lovers are resurrected years after the fact; burnt suppers are recalled with perfect clarity. Blaming someone else for a problem can feel so satisfying in the moment that it can be difficult to pause and see the damage being done. But, as this chapter will show, placing blame is a hollow victory.

THE CYCLE OF BLAME

In a lasting relationship, there are a myriad of opportunities to find fault with one another. Of course minor, commonplace issues will always arise: who got us lost this time, why he won't at least put the dishes in the sink, why she can't remember to fill the tank, and other such conflicts. More dangerous, however, are the long-standing problems between two individuals that can grow to monstrous proportions. The cycle of blame can then be bandied back and forth until it has eroded a once-strong love. Blame is in fact a habit, one that is all too easily summoned as life's unexpected twists and turns challenge our hearts to stay open.

That the unexpected will happen is a given. Feeling powerless in the face of uncertainty is universal. In such a moment of stress, blaming a loved one can offer a gratifying but fleeting feeling of power. This is an ironic twist because by blaming another for a problem, you are actually handing over your power. It is now up to that person to make your life either glorious or miserable.

Nothing you experience in life is *all* because of one person. Like the natural world that surrounds you, relationships are a system of interconnectedness, a complex web of personality and history. By blaming another, you take yourself—your understanding, empathy, and input—out of the mix and assign the control to someone else. You lose your connection to yourself and the other person and are often left feeling dependent, victimized, and powerless.

Blaming obscures the chance to learn from experience. You impede your emotional maturation as an adult when you explain to yourself that another person is the cause of your problems, instead of looking into your own influence on a social system, whether a marriage, family, or work group, in order to understand it better. Each of us brings along a mixed bag of positive and negative traits. By observing how both affect a relationship, you are able to learn from your mistakes and manage your own happiness.

How does this work, though, when you are on the frontlines of an imperfect love? When it's so tempting to scream and shout and pout as blame points its knobby finger at the boyfriend passed out on the couch or the spouse quickly hiding the credit card bill under the toaster? It *was* her fault, you may say. Maybe, but perfection eludes most of us. And it can be especially challenging to apply that truth to those you love. You probably tend to hold the ones closest to you to a higher standard, because you need them more, because you see their unacceptable traits more. Their behavior may also hold up a mirror to you, reflecting qualities in yourself that you reject. By virtue of their proximity you are privy to their darker sides, and can easily be disappointed by them. What is the other option, then, when blaming seems the only logical thing to do?

SHARING RESPONSIBILITY

The other choice is to take partial responsibility for the conflict at hand. This choice gives you a sense of control and the possibility of lasting happiness within a relationship that is certain to have bumps along the way. It also allows you to complete the task of growing up, as you develop new skills for handling conflicts that remind you of earlier times. Taking responsibility means pausing for a beat in a moment of stress and resisting the reactive urge to instantly blame the other party. It requires emotional centeredness and a fresh set of eyes that can take a step back and look at a situation with clarity and empathy.

Imagine that each birthday you have spent with your spouse is more disappointing than the last. Not once has he made a dinner reservation for a special evening, and his gifts are obviously picked up at the last minute on the way home from work. One year, he forgot entirely. Your initial reaction is to blame him. Why does he not understand how important this is to you; that not celebrating your birthday makes you feel unloved? How can he be so thoughtless time and time again when you always put in the effort to make *his* birthday special?

You've voiced your frustration, but he just doesn't get it. You are at an impasse. You blame him for hurting you, and this leaves you with little to no recourse. You remain angry, unsatisfied, and resentful.

What's worse, you now dread your birthday—something you looked forward to as a child—and the inevitable fight it brings each year.

A situation like this one can dim your happiness. Your dream outcome, that he one day has an epiphany and flies you to Fiji on your birthday, is out of your hands. But what you *can* choose is how *you* respond to your disappointment. By owning the part you play in your discontent, you have the power to redeem your happiness. Take another look at the possibilities. Perhaps his family didn't make a big deal about birthdays growing up. Maybe he resents feeling "forced" to show affection on one specific day out of the year and would rather surprise you on a random Tuesday. What if, in his eyes, your demand to be feted seems childish or slightly ridiculous?

Whatever the reason, your expectations are clearly out of sync. By realizing that his idea of showing affection is different from yours, you can let go of the blame and accept that he thinks differently from you on this particular issue. Unlike the quicksand of resentment, this option contains endless possibilities: You could instead take a trip with a girlfriend, suggest an intimate dinner at your favorite spot (with you making the reservation), or buy yourself that delicate bracelet you've had your eye on. Blame makes you a passive participant, while taking personal responsibility puts you in the driver's seat, able to take whatever steps are necessary to ensure your happiness.

JACKSON AND SUSAN

During much of their twelve-year marriage, Jackson and Susan have been locked in a cycle of blame. A match made in the moneyed corridors of Wall Street, they have successful careers in finance, and two thriving children. But despite their wealth and the riches of family life, over the years both have become desperately unhappy.

More than a decade earlier, Jackson had set his sights high for a marriage partner. He wanted to be in awe of the woman he would spend his life with; he wanted a striver like himself. And, in Susan, Jackson found just that. Their romance was fueled by their mutual ambition and a genuine respect for one another.

As the years went by, however, both noticed that their sex life was dwindling. At first, they assumed it was a symptom of busy schedules and stressful jobs. But when making love once a month became not at all, there clearly was a deeper problem. And when Susan admitted to Jackson that she was having an affair with a successful senior client, a cycle of blame began that threatened to implode their marriage. Jackson could barely grasp that his wife could sleep with another man. He felt betrayed and unsure that he could ever get over it.

From Jackson's perspective, the affair was a cruel irony. He had time and again complained to Susan that she rarely initiates sex. Even after a long day, he would lay in the dark hoping for some sign of her desire for him. Once her breathing deepened, he knew another chance for intimacy was gone. It hurt each time, but he buried his vulnerability beneath his anger and blamed her for not being a sexual person. Jackson began to think of her as less of a woman, frosty in the bedroom and manly as a partner.

Susan, however, sensed his verbal requests for sex as a demand, not an invitation. As their sex life deteriorated, she blamed him for eventually becoming chilly and withdrawn. They still loved each other deeply, but the barriers between them had disrupted their connection. Their mutual blame left them little room to re-establish their bond and led Susan to succumb to the amorous gestures of her client.

SHADOW CHILDREN AT PLAY

As is often the case, Jackson and Susan's behavior in this situation is a reflection of previous childhood pain. The lessons you learn when you are young are like shadows, drifting along beside you as you journey through adulthood. In Susan's case, she was disappointed in both of her parents, who she experienced as weak and ineffectual. As a child, they could not relate to a daughter who had such a spark. She felt abandoned, as they neglected to give her much direction. Susan responded by building up a system of defenses that protected her from showing how much she needed them. The woman the world now saw always acted as if she preferred a handshake to a hug. Her predatory client sensed Susan's need for a shoulder to lean on and seductively exploited her underlying hunger for affection. Similarly, Jackson's parents also placed responsibility on his shoulders at a young age. His father left for Florida when he was in grade school and started a whole new family, leaving his mom an overwhelmed single mother. Jackson, the "man of the house" at age ten, still feels that longing for a nurturing love that he missed in childhood and had hoped to find in his marriage.

Susan and Jackson's marriage was unraveling as both accused the other of destroying their chance for happiness. Their much-needed personal boundaries had been shattered; both felt victimized in an endless cycle of recrimination and blame. It was only when they began to take individual responsibility for the situation that they could start to rediscover their lost happiness.

A MARRIAGE SEEN THROUGH FRESH EYES

In order to save their relationship, Susan and Jackson both decided to take active steps to break free of their cycle of blame. They have committed themselves to seeing their situation with fresh eyes, and, little by little, are realizing the part each played in the other's failures. Susan has come to appreciate how her protective, self-defending style—learned as a child—pushes Jackson away emotionally, making it difficult for him to sexually connect. With this realization in place, she can begin to build a more permeable picket fence rather than a brick wall to maintain a feeling of safety with less need to attack. By looking at how she has contributed to their problems, she is avoiding the dead-end scenario of blame while at the same time empowering herself. Over time, this power will give her increasing courage to become emotionally vulnerable, which in turn will lessen Jackson's feelings of rejection.

Jackson is taking responsibility to be honest with Susan about how her cool manner and take-charge attitude make him feel. This is a very new move for him. By choosing to be open rather than obscuring his feelings, he is putting a boundary in place to keep his identity intact. Jackson sees now that blaming Susan and hiding from their problems only exacerbated his unhappiness and drove her into the arms of another man. As he witnesses Susan's glacial anger melting, his desire for her is rekindling. Susan and Jackson have initiated a new cycle, one in which each is responsible for their own happiness. Their marriage is more solid because of it.

By making the choice to take partial responsibility rather than to blame, you have the power to create your own happiness independent of your partner. Here are some steps you can take in a moment of stress to avoid blame:

1. **Stay in control.** Remind yourself that the momentary feeling of power that blame can give you is false and actually leaves you powerless.

2. **Get unstuck.** Blame can be a bad habit. Break the cycle any way you can: Walk away from a fight, meditate, or talk to someone new about the problem.

3. **Take a look through fresh eyes.** Force yourself to actively see a situation from the other person's point of view.

4. **Reverse the charges.** Take an honest look at how you contributed to the problem.

5. **Let it go.** Sometimes the only way to move past a problem is to consciously proceed forward. Don't hold on to your resentment.

Remember: These steps are the ideal. A life worth living puts us on a path where we strive toward our best way of being for a lifetime. The joy of living can be found in a perennial state of becoming.

Chapter 12

NEEDS VERSUS WANTS
Knowing What You Require to Be Satisfied

The struggle between giving in to your wants and understanding your needs has far-reaching implications. When you recognize the difference between the two, you take an important step in securing your happiness. So, what distinguishes a want from a need? Don't they both indicate something you desire for yourself? Yes, but while a want is transient and automatic, a need is something that is required for living a long, healthy, ethically consistent life.

Imagine the smoker: He *wants* to indulge in his post-meal cigarette, but he *needs* to take care of his body. Sounds simple enough, but for the smoker, this choice is laden with a mental cacophony of chemical addiction, shame, habit, enjoyment, and denial. He knows he needs to quit, but each time he puts flame to paper, he submits to a want that provides a momentary pleasure. Five minutes later, his feelings of self-recrimination return, and with them his customary low-grade pulse of dissatisfaction.

WHEN NEEDS ARE HIDDEN

Of course, there are few smokers—or other addicts—who don't recognize on some level the necessity of quitting. Acting on a need becomes more difficult, however, when you can't identify what it is that you require for long-term contentment. A good example is a busy working mother who cherished her solitude before starting a family. Now, three wonderful kids later, she cannot understand why she rarely feels content. Ashamed, she won't voice her unhappiness to her husband because it would seem ungrateful. She has forgotten that, in order to be at peace, she *needs* alone time to recharge. Once she recognizes this—and acts on it by taking an hour each day to go to the gym or read a book—she will have taken an important step toward true happiness.

Discovering what you require in order to live a satisfying life is an ongoing process. As you grow and change, certain needs become obvious based on your personality and experiences—your partner may be organized and need everything in its proper place; you may work best in an environment of virtual chaos. But your needs are many, and some can even be concealed from your consciousness. What happens when, like that busy mother, you don't know what you need? How do you distinguish between your wants—which bring instant gratification—and true needs, which bring enduring peace? Complying with your wants offers pleasure and transient satisfaction; meeting your needs offers you lifelong fulfillment and an experience of gratitude. This distinction can be especially difficult for shy people raised by self-absorbed parents. Taking a backseat to their parents' needs, those who grew up in this situation have difficulty recognizing their requirements in adulthood.

Furthermore, it is often the case that meeting a need is something you don't necessarily *want*. As the smoker knows, what your body—or mind or soul—requires to function at an optimal level can be diametrically opposed to what your reactionary, lazy, addicted, inner two-year-old wants. You may have a need for being financially solvent (it enhances your self-esteem and gives you a sense of control in an uncertain world), but this necessity can go by the wayside when you don't feel like cooking and instead lay down your Visa for $50 worth of takeout sushi. In such a moment, you don't want to meet your requirement, so you ignore it and succumb to the easier alternative.

PLAN TO OVERCOME SHORT-TERM WANTS

If you notice that a short-term want is overpowering a long-term need, treat yourself with kindness. Give yourself the benefit of the doubt that with patience and foresight, need will prevail over want. Using the sushi example, tomorrow on your way home stop at the supermarket and perhaps pick up a frozen dinner. If you notice that meets your need for saving money but not your need for a gourmet-tasting dinner, the next night buy some prepared salad, fresh bread, and perhaps some fish. Figure out how to make this purchase less than the cost of the original sushi meal. Helping a need to prevail over a want takes planning. This can be accomplished one small step at a time.

NEEDS VERSUS WANTS IN AN INTIMATE RELATIONSHIP

This Turning Point takes on yet another dimension when you add a loved one (and his or her needs and wants) to the mix. One of the primary themes of this book is that we all arrive at an intimate relationship with our bags packed full of personal traits and histories.

Our individual needs, like water to rock, have shaped our lives. If your mate doesn't understand and agree with what you require—and vice versa—long-term love can be challenging. Obviously a new love's path is made smoother by whatever needs are shared: *We both need constant companionship! We are committed vegans!*

In the context of understanding wants versus needs, there are three scenarios in which interpersonal difficulties may arise:

1. When one partner confuses his wants for needs
2. When one partner does not relate to and therefore does not respect the other's needs
3. When the needs of one or both partners are unconscious or unknown

Let's imagine you are grappling with the first scenario. It's January and a friend calls saying he has scored last-minute tickets from his boss to go to the Super Bowl. You don't particularly care about the teams that are playing, but this is an offer you can't pass up. All your college buddies will be there; it will be a great chance to reconnect, a prospect that has become increasingly difficult since everyone has moved away and started families.

Excited, you race home to tell your wife, whom you fully expect will be thrilled at your luck. And she is, until she looks at the calendar and frowns. You have been trying unsuccessfully for two years to conceive and there is a good chance that Super Bowl weekend will coincide with when she next ovulates. She tells you this in a neutral tone, allowing you to make your choice. "We'll catch it the next month, honey," you say, as you go online to book your ticket.

You have chosen a want (going to the Super Bowl) over a need (building a family). And at this point, you don't even recognize it. In fact, although you do want to have children, you feel that your need at this point in time is to be with your friends and enjoy yourself. In the moment, it is easy to justify this decision: Maybe her cycle will be off a day or two. You work hard and deserve a vacation. What difference will one month make? Whatever you say to yourself will possibly carry no water a few months later when, after another disappointing pregnancy test, your wife explodes in a fury of resentment. She will say that she feels so alone and that you aren't truly by her side on this difficult fertility journey. And she may cite your boozy football weekend with your buddies as evidence of your emotional and physical abandonment. Is this fair? Does it matter? Certainly, all miscommunications are reparable, and going to the Super Bowl is not a crime. But, when you mistook your want for a need, you made a choice that fueled tension between you and your wife.

Recognizing and acting on what you need—even if it means making the choice to support long-term goals at the expense of short-term pleasure—helps to sustain a lasting love. If both partners strive to distinguish and live according to their needs, it provides an umbrella of contentment over the relationship, a feeling of teamwork and shared goals. Abraham Maslow's hierarchy of needs, from his well-known work *Toward a Psychology of Being*, categorizes needs into five ascending groups (usually depicted in a pyramid): Physiological, Safety, Love/Belonging, Esteem, and Self-actualization. The first two support physical well-being. Once basic needs are met, people have the freedom to focus on the upper tiers, which define personalities. Wise action can lead to fulfilling these innate needs, making people happier and more fully able to connect with a loved one.

JASON AND LISA

Jason and Lisa's bickering stems from not understanding and therefore not respecting each other's needs. The subject of their most recent battle was Jason's university colleague, Helena. For a time, Jason denied his ongoing friendship with Helena, as he knew the fact that they were former lovers would make Lisa uncomfortable. This all changed when Lisa ran into Helena at the local playground one day. Their kids being the same age, the two women began chatting. Helena was quick to say how much she appreciated Jason's help in moving her and her son into their new apartment. Lisa just nodded and smiled and was relieved when her daughter stubbed her toe and ran over seeking solace. Seething inside, but with a friendly wave, she said goodbye to Helena and headed home.

Confronting Jason with her playground revelation, Lisa watched, arms crossed in righteous anger, as her husband first denied having any kind of relationship with Helena. Seeing she wasn't going to believe him, he quickly changed tactics and went on the offensive. "Who are you to dictate who I spend my time with? If you don't know how to trust me, that's not my problem."

"'Who am I?' I'm your wife," she responded. "And I would appreciate it if you would refrain from pursuing a friendship with your very attractive, single, former lover!"

They left it at that, with Jason feeling that she was trying to control him and Lisa sinking into a deep hole of mistrust. And she was right to sense that something was amiss in her marriage, although Helena was not the real issue. Jason did have a secret—an addiction to cocaine that he felt helped him get through his daily lectures and endless faculty meetings. His reliance on the drug filled him with shame, but he felt he could not admit his weakness to Lisa, fearing she would use it against him in the long battle their marriage had become.

Jason and Lisa needed to find a way to create a safer emotional environment so that there could be more authentic sharing of fears and apprehensions. Both felt that when they opened up with some vulnerable piece of information, the other used it during a fight (Chapter 20 will explore the difference between fair and unfair fighting). This distance left them unable to brainstorm together to discover within a receptive setting what it is they truly need to be happy together.

A PERFECT STORM

Lisa has a need to trust Jason. But by pushing the limits of her trust (Helena) and keeping a damaging secret (cocaine), Jason does not support this need. What's worse, rather than being upfront with her husband about what she requires for happiness, Lisa confuses her need to trust him with her want to control him. She berates him, suspiciously asks where he's been, and looks for "evidence" in his desk and pockets when he's out of the house. None of these barrier-building behaviors facilitate a secure trust in their marriage.

Meanwhile, Jason is confusing his need for freedom with his want for secretive, damaging behavior. Jason's father was bipolar, making his childhood home a tense environment where the family took great pains not to upset Daddy. Worried about his difficult dad's needs, Jason never learned to recognize his own. Jason now needs to feel like his own man and live autonomously within his partnership with Lisa. Her suspicion makes this an unlikely prospect. Instead of preparing a protective canvas for himself and Lisa, one in which understanding and insight could lead to the verbalization of what he needs, he engages in secretive behavior in order to feel as if he's out from under her thumb.

FINDING A SAFE SPACE TO COMMUNICATE

Jason and Lisa's confusion over their needs and wants has created a perfect storm of dysfunction in their relationship. This couple's best chance of staying together will be creating a safe space for honest communication. Intimate listening (discussed in detail in Chapter 16) is crucial for discovering our own and our partner's needs. What are some strategies for achieving intimate listening if you are angry and full of distrust? If you are irritated and occupied with suspicion, you first have to work on yourself. Treat yourself with kindness, perhaps seeking the listening, compassionate ear of a friend or trained therapist to lighten your black emotions.

Without being able to cleanse your mind, it is almost impossible to hear out your partner's side of the story. And in the case of Jason this is a two-tiered challenge. First, Lisa has to offer the space to truly understand why Jason continues his friendship with

Helena. And then if Lisa really works at giving her partner the benefit of the doubt while owning the part that she plays in the nonreceptive atmosphere they have created, Jason would probably fly into her arms craving nothing more than to share his secret with Lisa and get some help.

Unlike wants, needs do not go away. If they are not met, things tend to fall apart. Making the choices that reflect your needs can result in a life well lived. In an intimate relationship, it is possible to reside in concordance with your own needs while supporting whatever your partner requires for his personal happiness. The trick is to gain enough wisdom along the way through intimate listening to recognize what is essential for each of us.

Chapter 13

DETACH VERSUS WITHDRAW
The Art of "Getting Across the Street"

Learning to detach from a loved one in a moment of conflict is crucial for nurturing a lasting relationship. In fact, the majority of the couples I encounter who eventually end up in divorce court have a fundamental confusion about this central Turning Point. If the decision to either detach or withdraw becomes muddled, love's dance falters and you watch helplessly as it falls apart. On the other hand, if you can learn to objectively look yourself in the eye by detaching in a moment of stress, you become a self-reflective witness of your own behaviors and emotions.

UNDERSTANDING THE DISTINCTION

A patient once described an image that perfectly represents the constructive choice of detaching: "getting across the street." Here's what happens. Those you are closest to will inevitably do something to offend. Getting across the street means that instead of instantly lashing out when he interrupts you at the dinner party or when she criticizes your driving *again*, you mentally and emotionally step away in order to disconnect from the situation at hand. By taking a moment (or a day or a month) for a cleansing breath, you are allowing a space to open up, permitting a better chance for clarity. Once your initial annoyance, anger, or disappointment fades, you are left with the power and curiosity to investigate what it was that your lover's actions triggered within you, examine what role or issue you are projecting onto him or her (an image embedded from your history), and begin the bridge-building action or conversation that will address the concern.

Detaching is a tool for self-awareness. Withdrawal, however, is analogous to crawling into a cave and hiding out in self-protection. When you choose to withdraw in a moment of stress (through impenetrable silence or physical or emotional absence), it has the effect on your partner of feeling abandoned, invisible, and/or invalidated. If your immediate goal is to get even for what you feel your partner has done to you, then you may have accomplished it by withdrawing. If your ultimate goal is lasting love, withdrawal creates a serious obstacle to accomplishing it.

Withdrawal is overattachment's dark sister. Falling in love is the slipperiest of slopes, and the plummet to feelings of "you are my everything" and "I can't live without you" can be swift. Although romantic at first glance, being overattached to a loved one is dangerous for a long-term relationship. It crushes the boundaries necessary for individual growth within a partnership. Without boundaries, when you are inevitably hurt or insulted by a loved one's actions, you lack the wherewithal to detach, instead withdrawing at the slightest offense, so emotionally raw are you.

The irony is obvious: Loving someone in the way a child loves a favorite bear or blanket (obsessed and unable to go on if it's left at the restaurant) can obliterate the very relationship you cherish.

BEHAVIORS OF DETACHMENT AND WITHDRAWAL

To an outside observer, the difference between detaching and withdrawing may not be immediately apparent. Both involve a stepping away from a loved one in a moment of empathic disconnect. The person on the receiving end of either detaching or withdrawal can tell the difference, however, because in detaching you are offering breathing room to figure out what occurred. On the other hand, when you withdraw, you are reacting to feeling overwhelmed and, perhaps unintentionally or not, punishing through abandonment.

Given the critical nature of this Turning Point, there are some behaviors—in both your partner and yourself—of which to become aware. Following is a table that shows four common behaviors for detachment and withdrawal, as enacted by the subject (the one who is exhibiting the behavior) and received by the object (the spouse or partner).

BEHAVIORS OF DETACHMENT AND WITHDRAWING

	Withdrawal	Detachment
Behavior/Feelings of the Subject	Eyes glaze over; Heart closes; Feelings of anger, resentment, defeat, and despair; Clueless to one's own behavior	Deep cleansing breath; Mind clears; Space to think; Benefit of the doubt; Witnessing your own behavior
Behavior/Feelings of the Object	Feels abandoned; Lonely; Helpless; Invisible	Feels heard; Appreciated; Loved; Seen

YOUR BRAIN ON DETACHMENT

Recent studies prove the connection between emotion and physiological responses in the brain. Daniel Siegel wrote an important book about this subject, *The Mindful Brain: Reflections and Attunement in the Cultivation of Well-being.* The difference between a functional MRI of a brain when one is feeling serene and the same scan when one is angered is striking. The limbic area of the brain stores your implicit memories and can become overwhelmed by your history. Without an intervention, it can become flooded with energy as neurons fire away, like gasoline thrown on a fire.

The accelerant here is the past. When you are upset by a lover's misstep, your anger or disappointment is the direct result of childhood memories being triggered. These emotional paths are well worn. You may not consciously remember feeling abandoned when Mom dropped you off at day care at two months old. But now, thirty years later, you experience that familiar sense of abandonment keenly when your husband stands you up for dinner. You become flooded with resentment, not fully understanding your extreme reaction, helpless as you relive the powerlessness of childhood again and again. You are projecting your mother's actions onto your unsuspecting husband. Though his "crime" is no doubt rude, by reacting with the full force of a lifetime of anger at Mommy, you both will walk away from this fight frustrated and confused.

Learning to detach can reprogram your brain. It allows you to become a witness to your own emotional reality, a split in consciousness Sigmund Freud described as the observing ego. You are on stage and in the audience at the same time, compassionately observing the child within that wants to scream, cry, or pout, while allowing your adult self to approach the situation with poised attentiveness.

HOW TO PHYSICALLY DETACH

By detaching in a moment of stress, your brain chemistry is actually altered. Often, physical activities can facilitate the mental discipline necessary for achieving this physiological change. If you've ever dreaded going to the gym only to emerge sweaty and happy, you'll recognize this phenomenon. There are many ways in which you can step away from a situation and break your emotional overload. Meditation and exercise—especially dance—are excellent "circuit breakers" that can clear one's mind. Deep breathing is also a simple and always available method for getting across the street from a loved one.

Although it may seem counterintuitive, moving your body is an important tool for maintaining emotional health. The two are linked, just as your sexual relationship contains elements of the physical as well as the emotional. The next time you find yourself ready to explode when your partner is rude, crude, or just plain impossible, remember that you have a choice. You can get up from the table, put on your sneakers while informing your partner that you are heading out to get a break from the argument, and briskly walk around the block, letting time, movement, and a bit of space give you some perspective. You are then assisting the neurons in your brain to reflect the new experiences that they are seeing. Or, you can slam your hands on the table, go into the den, and turn on the TV. Does the following scenario sound familiar?

"What's wrong?" he'll say.

"Nothing."

"It doesn't seem like nothing."

"Well, it is."

He'll stare at the back of your head for a moment, you'll turn up the volume, and out he goes, slamming the door. You withdrew; the connection is broken.

TRACY AND TOM

Tracy and Tom, a couple who is no longer together, exemplify the danger of withdrawing. Tom, a gentle, shy guy, was initially attracted to Tracy's ebullient personality. Always the life of the party, efficient at work and at home, Tracy was fiercely in control of her life. As the years passed and children arrived, Tracy became ever more competent, leading their small family forward like a very petite general.

Over time, Tom, a mere foot soldier in their lives, withdrew
to what he called his "brown chair." Every day after work Tom
would arrive home, smile at the children and his wife, eat dinner,
and retire to the brown chair in the far corner of their living room.
There he would remain, reading a book. Tracy imagined that Tom
was satisfied, a quiet man who required little. After all, whatever
she asked of him, he did. He supported his family, went to all
ceremonial events and weekly religious services, and was friendly
to her parents and siblings. Tracy was content. She imagined life
going on and on, until they were grandparents sitting on a porch
playing happily with their many grandchildren.

It was when Tom began an affair with Vicky, a consultant
whom he met through work, that things began to fall apart. After
every encounter with his lover, he felt shell-shocked and depressed
that he was capable of betraying his wife and possibly hurting
his kids. By the time they got to my office, Tom was envisioning
death as the only relief from his guilt and depression. He was hor-
rified at the thought of divorce, but the road back to a happy life
together was just too shattered. The cumulative effect of a decade
of withdrawing from his wife, of choosing the brown chair rather
than engaging her, even if it meant conflict, had left them virtual
strangers.

A GOOD DIVORCE?

Tom's great dread was becoming "Mr. Barbecue," which for
him meant a life that would never change and was forever predict-
able. Now, with the benefit of the two decades in which they have
been divorced, Tom realizes that his withdrawal was an intractable
reaction to Tracy's strong (bossy, in his eyes) personality and his
fear of becoming swallowed up by her.

But could they have saved their marriage? If Tom had been able
to detach from his feelings of being trampled by Tracy's big personality, he may have realized that his urge to retreat felt very familiar.
The child of two successful academics, Tom grew up intimidated by

his parents' aggressively intellectual nightly dinners, during which they would quiz him on the current events of the day. Being shy as well as introverted, young Tom wanted to sink beneath the floorboards under his mom and dad's expectant gaze. He suffered from being excessively put into the limelight and overstimulated by so much talk. In his marriage, unlike in his childhood, Tom did have the power to withdraw, and boy, did it feel good. Of course, the price was rather high. Had he detached and turned his gaze onto his own fraught past, he could have seen his wife more clearly as an individual, rather than a specter of all he endured as a child.

Both Tom and Tracy have gone on to enjoy successful relationships with other partners. Their children are grown and happy. Which brings us to an important question: Is there such a thing as a "good" divorce? As I hinted at the beginning of this chapter, of the couples I have counseled who ended their relationships, practically every one included at least one partner who was unable to detach from his or her spouse. In my experience, an inability to see who one's partner truly is, beyond the role projected onto him or her, has doomed more long-term relationships than has any other type of discord.

Ironically, in these cases, divorce may propel each member of the couple to uncover a more enlightened view of themselves. With time and space, they may understand that their union was predicated upon a fundamental lack of self-awareness that could only lead to a harmful pattern of blame and withdrawal. They can keep this bittersweet wisdom in mind for future—and hopefully happier—relationships.

Judith Wallerstein, psychologist and author of the famous study *The Unexpected Legacy of Divorce*, would disagree that there is such a thing as a good divorce once children are in the picture. It is true that breaking the foundation upon which a child relies is always traumatic. But a bad match between parents also contributes to a painful childhood for their offspring. So which is worse: divorce or unhappily staying together? According to Wallerstein, staying together avoids the deeply irreparable assault to the psyche that is the result of parents splitting up. Yet, many of my patients whose conflicted parents did not divorce dreamed that their perennially warring and mismatched parents would have gone their separate ways and brought peace to two homes instead of stress and conflict to one. This question of divorce is of course highly personal and dependent upon the specific situation.

> With care and attention, the distinction between detachment and withdrawal can become clear long before your relationship crumbles. And if crumbling is inevitable, perhaps you can learn from the plight of Bill Murray's character in the movie *Groundhog Day*. He woke up daily to the very same scene until he was able to change his own behavior. Once he realized the part he was playing in the repetition, the day changed.
>
> This Turning Point highlights a theme that you'll notice time and again in this book: It is only through changing ourselves (not our partners!) that a long-term love can survive. Detaching in a moment of stress allows the necessary space for self-reflection. Withdrawing, while tempting, opens no window for insight. Instead, we sit in the dark, grumbling and blaming and running in mental circles, powerless and alone.

Chapter 14

SPEAKING UP VERSUS SILENCE
Share Your Thoughts, Share Yourself

Undoubtedly, relationships would be simpler if you could read your partner's mind. Can't he just *know* I'd rather not spend my birthday with his parents? Do I have to *spell out* how I like to be touched in order to have an orgasm? Why must I *explain* to her that I'm terrified of looking for a new job? Speaking up can make you feel needy, embarrassed, too aggressive, too vulnerable. Hoping your partner will instead read your mind seems at first glance the less thorny path.

This Turning Point is related to desires originating in the first years of life. When you are in a long-term relationship, memories of infant love with your caregivers are triggered. Surrendering to a lover engages basic feelings of safety. Before language, you relied on others to intuit your needs. And it mostly worked—you were fed and kept warm and dry, despite your inability to verbalize your desires. Because of this early association, there are times when you wish your lover could just read your mind like your first love objects did.

A VERBAL MISMATCH

Silence can have negative consequences in an intimate relationship. Besides risking the real possibility of being misunderstood, hitting the mute button on your desires can eventually result in an angry explosion when your unwitting partner is deaf to your soundless pleas. When you're frustrated by the weeks—or years!—of unmet needs, anger inevitably swoops in like a hurricane, leaving in its wake love's ruins. Frustration will find an outlet, whether through self-destructive behavior (such as an eating disorder or depression) or putting a fist through a wall. A community of isolated farmers in Norway—a culture not known for its loquaciousness—has its own solution. After the long, dark winter months spent only with their small family group, rather than risk conflict by voicing their desires, they walk across the frozen fields to yell at and share their dark emotions with the nearest mountain.

Most of us don't have a mountain to yell at and, although it's sometimes tempting, we would look nutty screaming or crying at an office building or a Starbucks in frustration. So how do you resolve this dilemma if one partner is uncomfortable speaking up and the other is not? Or, worse and not uncommon, what happens when *both* people are shy about verbalizing needs? Look at the following table and decide into which category you fall.

FOUR VERBAL TENDENCIES

Speaking up as a barrier: Taking all of the space, saying nothing personal, addicted to the limelight.	**Staying silent as a barrier:** A verbal introvert, offering space but not yourself, saying little that is personal, being averse to the limelight.
Speaking up as a boundary: Being a verbal extrovert, revealing authentic feelings, noticing when the other person may need floor time.	**Staying silent as a boundary:** Preferring to speak little, but when you do, speaking from the heart.

OUTGOING TYPES

If you're comfortable with verbal interaction, communicating your thoughts and needs seems natural and right. If you are open and often entertaining, you've probably been rewarded throughout your life with attention and laughter. However, being in an intimate relationship with a quiet person can have positive or negative consequences, depending on how you approach this difference.

If there is a problem with loving the spotlight, it is that you can be blinded by it. And if your partner is reserved, she could retreat even further while your show goes on and on and on. You may say, "But she loves that I make her laugh!" or, "If I stopped talking, we would be sitting in silence." Perhaps, but pay attention to how people around you react to your talkative manner. Are you outspoken to better share yourself with others and to draw them out, or does maintaining all eyes on you possibly fulfill a huge appetite for attention? When you are talking, do you leave space for interjection or do your audience's eyes glaze over a bit? Do you recognize when to provide room for another's voice?

NON-OUTGOING, SILENT, OR SHY TYPES

For others, speaking up for themselves on occasion, or interrupting another person to do so, can feel like walking naked down Fifth Avenue. So what is the quiet person's loved one to do? Stillness puts the burden on the more verbal partner to draw out his or her lover, to fill a gap. This may seem strained or contrived, but is actually a challenging gift. You could spend another evening resenting the weight of keeping the conversation going, or consciously choose to focus on your lover, letting receptive silence replace your chatter, or probe his or her thoughts through attentive inquiry. Providing an opportunity for your lover to speak demonstrates curiosity about what she thinks and feels. Sensing this, she is more likely to risk opening up. Often a quiet person has fascinating thoughts and feelings, having spent serious time developing them. Naturally good listeners, they have absorbed a lot while the rest of us babbled on.

Consider the Western world's creation story. In the Bible, the first sentence commences: "In the beginning God created the heaven and the earth. . . ." The word used for God in this instance is *Eloheim* (in Hebrew), which is a contraction of the singular *El*, meaning "Deity" and the majestic plural suffix *–im*. Interpreters of the Bible have concluded that *El* would have been sufficient to identify the name of the almighty, and since each word in the Torah has many meanings and none are accidental, using the contraction *Eloheim* suggests that God contracted to make room for mankind.

There are hundreds of words for God in the Old Testament, each with its own specific meaning, but the first time it is used, it is presented in the form of a contraction. Why? If God is everywhere and perfect, then in order for man to come into being, what must God do? Offer space; contract. This ancient lesson is a core element of loving.

THE TROUBLE WITH SILENCE

Keeping your thoughts to yourself can serve to either support or tear down a relationship. Although you may be shy (fearful of risks) or introverted (easily overwhelmed by too much stimuli), this does not mean everyone should sit patiently at your feet, penny in hand, hoping for your thoughts. Innate reticence can feel like rejection to your companion. Offering little of yourself can not only cause discomfort, but also may be experienced either as an intentional or unintentional instrument of control, a power play that builds a barrier to real connection. After all, if you say nothing, you will never be wrong; no one can judge you. It could appear to a companion that while she chatters on, freely giving out information that may make her vulnerable, you stay quiet and secure knowing there's no chink in your armor.

That said, how can those who are less vocal keep up their end of the proverbial conversation? Being and staying in love requires a leap of faith—a trust—mainly in yourself, that you can safely voice your private thoughts and feelings. And if you feel you are being intentionally or inadvertently ridiculed or punished for them, you can clue in your clueless partner that his behavior hurts. Keeping a love alive does not mean you need to match your more verbal lover word-for-word, but it does mean paying attention when a space opens up within your own heart. Move to interject yourself. Don't wait for him to read your mind or for an opportunity; know that interrupting is basic to existence, and waiting means you may be waiting forever. Instead, push yourself to give what you can of yourself.

If you are a more silent type in a long-term relationship, imagine the way you feel in the ocean when you are swimming against the current. It is hard to do, but the effort pays off. Over a lifetime, opening up to another despite your continuing resistance makes the relationship exciting and forever new, and develops muscle power in the form of sustained emotional strength.

SARAH AND SAMUEL

Dinner at the Greens' was like going to a performance where Samuel was the star. A towering man, Samuel ruled his wife and three teenage children, believing that everything that came out of his mouth was right and true. Sarah was a quiet woman who spent the first thirty years of their marriage at times frustrated, but generally resigned to taking a backseat to her husband's garrulousness. After all, he was smart and funny and she believed he had their best interests at heart.

This pattern could have continued indefinitely had their middle son, Jeffrey, not contracted a mysterious case of laryngitis his sophomore year of college. For months, all he could do was whisper. He and his parents went to every hospital and physician they could find to uncover the cure to this calamity. Finally, Jeffrey left for a semester abroad in Australia—a decision Samuel opposed, feeling that an American education was superior to anything taught abroad. While living thousands of miles from home, Jeffrey's voice eventually returned.

The decision to study abroad was the first time Jeffrey had opposed his father. His stance literally gave him back his voice. Upon returning home, however, Jeffrey reverted to the pattern of his mother and sisters—keeping quiet to avoid conflict with Samuel. The maturity and knowledge gained from his travels was under wraps. Speaking up about his burgeoning views on the world could only invite his father's ridicule, the thought of which took his breath away.

Sarah watched the light she saw in Jeffrey when he got off the plane slowly dim. It broke her heart to realize that all these years of silence had done a disservice to their children. She realized that she had chosen marital peace over her son and daughters' well-being. What had she taught them? To swallow their true voices? To sublimate their desires in order to avoid conflict with someone more verbal? It was time for a change.

THE GREENS MAKE SPACE

Sarah began to gradually suggest that Samuel speak less around the children and give them room to express themselves. At first, he had little awareness of why his normally passive wife was complaining after all of these years. Frankly—and he wasn't afraid to say so—he wondered if she was showing signs of early senility. Unused to being challenged in his own home, Samuel resisted mightily her suggestion that he was a bully.

Extremely uncomfortable with her newfound voice, Sarah knew that the reason she was pushing herself was that her children required her to be their advocate. She came up with a concrete plan to enhance family communication, thinking that Samuel would respond best to a "system." Dinnertime, which had been Samuel's domain, would now be sliced up into five-minute increments during which each family member would discuss anything of their choosing—their day, current events, even feelings. The rule was that this time allotment was to be a safe space where there would be no ridicule, no sarcasm, and no interruptions.

The experiment got off to a slow start, with Samuel biting his tongue and the rest of the family laboriously overcoming their shyness at this chance to speak up. But, as the months passed, something surprising happened. Samuel began to look forward to hearing his family's thoughts and feelings. By finally listening, he realized he was actually getting to know these people—and he liked them!

STRATEGIES FOR BUILDING SPACE

Sarah's example is just one real-life strategy for reining in someone who speaks too much—and for drawing out those who speak too little. Samuel needed a system that forced him to sit back and listen to those around him. Conversely, his quiet family also fared well from this type of structure, in which a specified time was created for them to express themselves. Someone who is an obsessive talker is using language as self-protection just as a silent person uses *not* talking as protection. However, having empathy for the talker's fear (masked by words) can help the quiet person to have some compassionate understanding of what she is up against while trying to influence her more loquacious other half to share the total talking time. Sarah knew Samuel's fears of losing control, of being found out to be not as great a man as he hoped to be. Establishing a structured "game" allowed him to save face and get comfortable being more authentically revealed without his characteristic forms of control.

If your partner tends to be unforthcoming (secretly hoping you'll read his mind), you can pray for psychic powers, or you can create a space for him to speak. Frame a conversation with specific questions, reiterating to him that whatever he says will be received in good faith. A willingness to endure sometimes-uncomfortable silence shows that you are patient and prepared to listen. Carving out a formal weekly "date" or monthly Saturday spent together can also let your partner know that these are occasions when sharing thoughts and feelings is not only appropriate, but also welcomed. I work with one couple who schedules what they coined their "State of the Union" date every six months in order to discuss areas in which each feels their relationship is thriving, and where it could use improvement. In such a structured setting, each comes with the expectation of give-and-take communication.

This entire book is laced with the importance of creating space for yourself as well as for another. To do this, you have to gain awareness that there is enough within you to welcome both taking and sharing the limelight, feeling full rather than empty. And, ironically, making room for someone who has difficulty taking their fair share of the total talking time is an empowering act of loving kindness that enhances your own well-being.

Conversely, if you are someone who finds it difficult to speak, what better way to demonstrate your dedication to a loved one than doing what is challenging? Push yourself to take a fair share of the talking time. By doing this, you unlock a gateway to an exciting life in which you and your partner can regularly contribute and learn.

(Painful shyness in adulthood is a topic that I researched for ten years, which culminated in *The Shy Single*, published in 2004 by Rodale Books.)

Chapter 15

GIVING THE BENEFIT OF THE DOUBT VERSUS MAKING ASSUMPTIONS
The Danger of Jumping to Conclusions

How would you feel if I assumed that you picked up this book because you cheated on your mate and now you want to find a way back to a loving partnership? Am I right? Probably not. In all likelihood, your situation is not something easy to guess. My making assumptions would not only be reckless; it could also elicit a defensive reaction: *That's not it at all! You've got me pegged all wrong.*

Making assumptions about people—their motivations, their actions in your absence, their private thoughts—is precarious guesswork. It's also usually incorrect, given the fact that individuals are moving targets, forever changing in surprising and sometimes contradictory ways. In an intimate relationship, the inclination to make assumptions about a loved one can feel irresistible. After all, you know your partner! You know why he didn't pick up when you called (he was probably on the phone with his horrible mother). You know why she was late (she is careless about time). We all think we know. In reality, we read one another based on our own narrow view of the world.

TRADING IN OUR ASSUMPTIONS FOR THE BENEFIT OF THE DOUBT

When you assume something about another person, you are choosing to project your own momentary feelings onto them. It is a reactive behavior that takes the place of checking in with a loved one to uncover the unpredictably complex individual he or she is. Making assumptions traps another person into a box you have created. Giving the benefit of the doubt, however, means that you confront your automatic assumptions, allowing that a loved one may confound your expectations. As the expression implies, there is a "benefit," a reward that comes out of giving it. By inquiring into what's going on, you can, together with your partner, discover the identifiable human emotions behind any behavior. This approach demonstrates a generosity of spirit from which both people profit.

Of course, not every assumption is wrong, and giving someone the benefit of the doubt won't sidestep all conflict. You may be right in assuming that your partner didn't mow the lawn because he felt lazy that day. And, you may give her the benefit of the doubt that she didn't show up for your son's play because of work only to find out that she wasn't working late after all. But, over time, a propensity toward either choice in this Turning

Point can have important repercussions. If you have a tendency to make assumptions about a loved one, you probably do hit the nail on the head every once in a while. But learning what is behind feeling "lazy" or why she left work early but did not come right to the play can build a new bridge to an old relationship. Imagine years of guesswork applied to someone who is ever-changing and growing. The cumulative wrong suppositions create a gap between who you *think* your mate is and the reality of who he or she *actually* is. And it defeats the possibility of discoveries that keep your relationship fresh.

On the other hand, over time, giving someone the benefit of the doubt allows you to see a more accurate version of who your partner is continuously becoming. In this scenario, will yourself to respond with thoughtful awareness. Instead of reflexively reacting from a place of anger or suspicion, take a step back and think about the many possibilities of what could really be going on. Maybe he *is* too lazy to cut the lawn. You can stew and run around in angry mental circles, recalling all the other instances when he has disappointed you. But when he mentions later in passing that he simply decided to wait to cut the grass because the lawn was wet, all your inner turmoil will have been for naught. And anyway, why judge someone you love rather than understand what is going on, even if laziness had been the truth of the matter?

FAMILY ARCHETYPES

Making assumptions about others is rooted in everyone's original family, where there is a tendency to stereotype one another. This categorization is a shorthand in order to see each other as unique, although the approach often backfires and ultimately obscures the very thing that was being attempted, which is to recognize each person's individuality. Are you the "funny one," the "responsible one," the "screwup"? Birth order and personality shore up these simplistic characterizations, all of which undermine the recognition of your more idiosyncratic adult development. Trapped in the typecasts of youth, it can feel like a Herculean effort to break free and prove that you were—and are—a multifaceted individual.

These myths tend to be reinforced when you see relatives during holidays and at other family gatherings. God forbid you get teary when given a sentimental gift. "She always was so *sensitive*," your mother says to the group, shaking her head ruefully. While it may be true that you have a softer side, her implication of weakness is maddening—and impossible to disprove. Should you take that moment to describe your recent toughness during a negotiation at work, or your refusal to back down to your bullying landlord, you only prove her point. "See, what did I tell you?" she continues. "Relax, darling. Don't be so defensive."

When you are assigned a negative category by an important other, you tend to react by overcorrecting. So, the investment banker whose parents were disappointed when she quit the ice-cream shop at age sixteen now works eighteen-hour days and wonders why she's unhappy. "Don't be a quitter!" her dad said at every graduation. "As a kid she just never could stick with anything, but look at her now," her mom tells her bridge group. Being categorized runs the risk of robbing you of the ability to have that specific human quality in your repertoire—in this case, knowing when to stop and relax.

CONFOUNDING THE PATTERN

When you become conscious of the stereotype that was placed upon you in childhood, you increase your chance of breaking free of these unintentionally held assumptions and revealing yourself as you truly are. You hope that the person you fall in love with will appreciate and encourage you to express yourself in all your complex, multifaceted glory, as you anticipate encouraging him in all of his contradictions. The danger of making assumptions about a long-term partner is that it repeats the old pattern of placing him into a reduced characterization. As a child, you were powerless and therefore a victim of the assumptions of your family. If, in your mature relationships, you are unable to break out of the habit of putting loved ones into fixed categories, the consequences are judging, blaming, and assuming that their behavior is because they are somehow fundamentally sneaky, or selfish, or naive. As time goes by, both partners become, in each other's minds, caricatures of who they really are. This treacherous path can take years to recover from and requires a virtual deprogramming of entrenched beliefs.

Giving people the benefit of the doubt shatters your instinct to classify objects as well as people. It offers breathing room to take a step back and see your loved ones for who they really are. This more open-minded approach supports your quest for finding joyful experiences as you continue to discover the evolving person she is becoming, instead of living day after day with someone whose inner life you think you know, but about which you can actually only guess.

RUTHIE AND ROB

Ruthie and her husband, Rob, together for three years and married for six months, are both on their second marriages. They have a beautiful baby boy, Nikolai. Ruthie supports their family as a high-end hair colorist; Rob is barely scraping by as a dentist. He maintains that the current health care system thwarts his efforts to earn a pay grade he deserves. He also blames depression for his lack of motivation, which prevents him from arriving at the office before noon.

Ruthie begins her day at 6:30, when she gives the baby his first feeding as Rob dozes on in bed. Getting ready for work, Ruthie pokes Rob under the covers as she walks by to reach her closet. She reminds him to take the car in, as the oil needs changing. "And don't forget—you promised to follow up with that practice in Morristown. It sounded like it could be a good spot for you." Rob, not answering, puts a pillow over his head as the hair dryer begins its predawn screech. As soon as she heads out the door, mumbling to herself that he'll probably get nothing done, Rob emerges from his cocoon. He revels in the silence and goes to pick up baby Nikolai. Father and son cuddle as they watch a Dora video together before the nanny comes at 9:00.

It is no great leap to understand Ruthie's frustration with her husband, as he lies prone on the bed. From her perspective, there is just too much to do for her to coddle him and leave him a sweet "honey-do" list that she assumes he won't take seriously. Her patience with his depression, and with his lack of organizational skills, which hinders his professional success, are near an end. So, what are Ruthie's options besides a daily dose of nagging and a staunch refusal to offer him the benefit of the doubt? Is there another way to get the results she wants?

The fact is, love is not a results-oriented game. Ruthie may never transform Rob into the man she wishes he were. Rob is who he is, and she knew this going into the marriage. His long history of owing money to friends and relatives, of not being able to support himself, was no secret. Ruthie is not going to change him, and neither could his ex-wife or the many therapists he has seen before and since. So, what is she to do? Just swallow all of the major and minor glitches in their relationship? Yes and no.

Giving Rob the benefit of the doubt would allow her to see him as a human being—not just a lump in the bed. If she could forgo her assumptions that Rob is going to sleep in *again*, and will likely fail to update his resume, it would help Ruthie to feel kinder to her husband. This friendlier thought can help her to remember why she was attracted to Rob in the first place and remind herself that the qualities she admired three years ago are still there. He is a committed companion; he supports her need for independence and makes her laugh. And, he provided her with a son in her forty-third year with the help of two in vitro fertilization treatments. Rob is a good father. Doesn't that trump occasionally sleeping in? If she wants her marriage to last, the answer must be yes.

Ruthie can only take charge of her perception of the situation. Following are six steps that Ruthie—and you—can take in order to transform making assumptions into giving the benefit of the doubt.

HOW TO OFFER THE BENEFIT OF THE DOUBT

To live in harmony with someone you believe is a frustrating partner, do the following exercise:

1. Make a list of *his* five *best* qualities.
2. Put them on your bathroom mirror.
3. Make a list of *your* five *worst* qualities.
4. Put them on your bathroom mirror.
5. Read each list once in the morning and once in the evening.

You have completed this exercise when you can replace frustration toward him with gratitude that he chooses to live with you despite your five frustrating qualities.

SOLUTIONS

Determined to keep her marriage on solid ground now that she has experienced gratitude, Ruthie suggested that maybe Rob needs more structured days to keep his motivation primed. They decided together to have the nanny only come in the afternoons, relying on Rob to take care of their son during the morning hours. Besides saving them money, this gives Rob the advantage of starting each day with a strong dose of love and the feeling of being needed—good medicine for his depression. And, by giving Rob the benefit of the doubt that he is doing his part, Ruthie feels that they are now more equal partners in providing for their small family.

> The decision to give a loved one the benefit of the doubt is a dynamic act of investing in your relationship. In the beginning, when you were falling in love and your partner could do no wrong, you were "all in," eager to believe that he or she was acting in your best interest. As time passed and mistakes were made, however, it may have become more difficult to conjure up that original inclination. The French philosopher Blaise Pascal suggested, in what is famously known as Pascal's Wager, that although it may be impossible to prove God's existence with reason, one has everything to gain and nothing to lose by believing. So it is with benefit of the doubt: It risks nothing and opens the door to the possibility of lasting love.

Chapter 16

INTIMATE LISTENING VERSUS HEARING

Listening with an Open Heart

If you appreciate the difference between painting by numbers and creating a piece of art that reflects the soul, you already understand how greatly hearing and intimate listening differ. We are all guilty of lending half an ear to the daily exchange of information in our households. And, often, merely hearing one another is sufficient for conveying that the dishes are clean or the dog is out. But this basic exchange of facts often goes in one ear and out the other and is little more than rote. Think about it: Today's voice recognition software can "hear" you. Do you want to be married to it?

Inevitably, merely hearing one another runs into a snag when one person hears what is literally being conveyed, but not what is happening beneath the surface. Everyone knows the difference between hearing and listening when *you* want to be understood. How do you feel when you have something important, or even trivial, that you wish to communicate to your partner as he sits on the couch right beside you, yet a million miles away? "I *heard* you," he will say when you attempt to disengage him from the TV or computer. This is maddeningly true, especially if he repeats back to you verbatim what you just said. But you know that you are not receiving that which you really crave: to be *listened* to.

GOING BENEATH THE SURFACE

Intimate listening is connecting to one another on a deeper level in order to achieve a soul connection. It is an active effort to understand what is truly going on in your partner's emotional life. The challenge of intimate listening is that people are not like books. You cannot open your lover to page one and discover a linear story that explains his behavior. More likely, you will be presented with clues you can mine through intimate listening until you strike upon his unique truth. For example, imagine you and your family vacation each summer with your parents at their beach house. For the past five years, your wife has spent these weeks grumpy or listless, going on long antisocial beach walks. She has told you repeatedly that she would rather use your minimal vacation time at a resort, away from extended family. And, though you hear her and think you understand her complaint (she can't really relax around the in-laws), you dismiss it as trivial, considering how much money you save by staying free of charge.

What might you discover if you look beneath what your wife is telling you? It is unlikely that she will—unprompted—reveal that spending so much time with your intact family highlights how broken her own family is. She may not even realize that this is why she feels a sense of dread in the weeks leading up to what should be a happy time. It is only through patient listening that this truth may emerge, resulting in an empathic connection.

Interestingly, by connecting to another's humanity, you actually engage your own. While merely hearing someone allows you to follow the path of least resistance, intimate listening requires that you focus on the hidden realities that exist within both your partner and yourself. This happens almost automatically, because when you lend a tolerant ear to a loved one, there is an increased chance for a shared connection. Continuing the example of the beach house, once you have reached the heart of the matter—that your family's togetherness reminds your wife of everything she lost when her parents divorced—you literally feel her pain by conjuring up your own understanding of loss, the ache of which is universal. Her story may remind you of being a child and moving away from all of your friends, or losing a beloved pet. Whatever it is, by mirroring her pain, you now have a deeper understanding of your wife and feel an alliance that comes from true compassion.

WHY IS INTIMATE LISTENING DIFFICULT?

The emotions you uncover through intimate listening tend to be of the uncomfortable sort. After all, you wouldn't bother to bury the shame, disappointment, or confusing dark memories of childhood if they didn't threaten your adult equilibrium. But these feelings are always present, bubbling just beneath the surface and affecting your behavior in nonproductive ways. If your partner's simplistic explanation that he ate the entire box of doughnuts in one sitting is "because I was hungry, dammit," it may be easier to take him at his word. Sitting down (after he's passed through his sugar high and inevitable low) and attempting to get to the bottom of his gluttony will be rough at best. He probably doesn't want to talk about the shame he felt being the "fat kid" growing up, unable to resist the comfort of sweets. And you certainly don't want the responsibility of connecting to his lingering humiliation. You have your own painful memories of acne-filled teenage years, thank you very much.

So why do this to yourself? Can't you just let the past be the past? The truth is that the past is never just the past. It is in us and around us and—if you let it remain out of your conscious awareness—it can control your life like a careless puppet master. Intimate listening is the necessary, if sometimes tender, emotional "operation" that provides the self-knowledge to manage life wisely. As crucial as regular visits to the dentist, intimate listening has beneficial long-term outcomes. It empowers you, and, whether you are the listener or the one being listened to, it offers a more insightful connection between partners.

ANITA AND ADAM

Anita keeps a meticulous family calendar on the computer in the living room. Its original purpose was to be an organizational tool to help the family stay on track. In actuality, the calendar has become a source of contention between Anita and her husband, Adam.

A typical conflict occurred one Sunday when Anita and her daughter came downstairs in spring dresses only to find Adam standing in the kitchen in his sweats. One look from his wife and he knew he was in trouble. "I told you a month ago that today was the family picnic," she said harshly. "All you had to do was look at the calendar!"

Adam was hurt and bewildered. "I honestly forgot. I thought it was sometime this summer," he said. He went to take a shower, while Anita, mumbling and cursing to herself, threw food and wine and other items into the picnic basket. *I am sick of having to remind him ten times for any date that includes him. It is like he is a visitor, not a family member, a partner. Oh, I hate him.*

How could Anita and Adam become proficient at intimate listening instead of just hearing each other, and then walking away in frustration? Anita has heard Adam frequently complain that he cannot decipher her computer calendar. She has heard even more times that Adam feels there is never space in the schedule for him to pursue his own fun. In response, Anita points to their ten-year-old, who reads her calendar easily and never has to ask her what is happening on any given day. And didn't she watch the kids last weekend when he wanted to meet a friend for lunch?

Both Anita and Adam feel that what each partner says about reading the calendar is ridiculous. Do you often prove to your spouse that what she says makes no sense at all? Do you often rely on "just the facts"? This rational approach to hearing another person is endemic to almost every couple I have ever met. At least one person in the twosome is a fact worshiper who sees no sense in getting all confused by emotions. It is what it is; the facts speak for themselves. The problem with this approach is that truly understanding what is going on with your partner, such as why he is distressed over something as simple as reading the calendar, requires a journey into much more than facts. It requires a willingness to participate in intimate listening. Adam and Anita must begin a journey of patience and mutual understanding.

THE SEVEN STEPS OF INTIMATE LISTENING

Following is an example of how to engage your partner in intimate listening.

1. Notice if there is a moment of empathic disconnect between you and your partner. For example, if he says, "You never help me get our taxes in order," your first thoughts may be, *Who does all of the expenses? Me. Who found the accountant? Me. Who hardly ever buys anything for herself? Me.* Keep these thoughts to yourself and proceed to Step Two.

2. Clear your mind. Take a deep cleansing breath, or many. If you are still annoyed, turn on some music and dance, or go

for a quick walk—physical movement clears your brain of accumulated memories that cause foggy thoughts. Again, this step is detaching, or "getting across the street."

3. In a neutral manner, repeat your partner's statement to him. Use his words but with a question mark at the end, indicated by your tone. "So, you feel I never help you get our taxes in order? How come you see it that way?" (Note that *how* works better than *why*. *Why* could sound like a challenge when you mean to show genuine open-minded curiosity as to *how* he sees the situation.)

4. Follow his line of thinking by repeating a sentence that has emotion in it. Do not change his words. His language is the key to his emotions. He may say, "I have been sitting in the basement for the last week trying to get all of the papers together, and you never ask me if you can help." A good way to respond is, "I never ask if I can help? If you experience [a set prefix] *that I never ask if I can help* [his words], how does that affect you [a set suffix]?" (Over the years, I have found that this formula of structuring the beginning and the end of the sentence with *If you experience,* then selecting a difficult-to-listen-to part of the speaker's sentence, and then ending the sentence with *how does that affect you,* gives both the listener and the speaker the opportunity to part the curtains and go deeper into why the speaker came up with the thought he is exploring. This thought usually has some resonance with experiences from his past.) You are not agreeing or disagreeing with his statement. You are merely using the set prefix and suffix to initiate the journey with him. Imagine you are in the ocean, scuba-diving at ten-foot intervals ever deeper beneath the surface as you continue listening and repeating the emotions he is verbalizing. You will see something new at each level; perhaps your partner reveals that he feels

lonely or is scared that the family won't be able to pay the taxes on time this year.

5. Reach for the past. When you feel he is revealing a vulnerable emotion (one that could also have been felt at an earlier life stage) you may ask him, "Do you remember a time earlier in your life when you were very little, that you felt you might not be able to complete a project and that no one was helping? Not your mother, your father, no grandparent, no sibling?" At that point, he may say, "You know, there was never anyone to help. My parents were too old, and my brothers were away from home by the time I was born. My house was a pretty lonely place to grow up."

6. Recognize an "aha" moment. You now realize why your partner was so miserable in the basement for the last week. It brought back memories of his lonely childhood, where he felt he had to forge ahead in the big world all by himself.

7. Build a bridge to him. At this point, he is no longer an "it," a difficult irrational pain in the neck; he is a "thou," your sweetie, whose painful memories from childhood pop up every now and then in a form that usually starts with him accusing you of some form of neglect. You could now say something like, "It was not my intention to neglect you in the basement. From my point of view, I believed that you wanted uninterrupted time to concentrate and complete the project. I in no way meant to abandon you. I was trying to support you, but my attempt unintentionally backfired. Do you believe me?" If he says yes, then you have completed all seven steps.

At first, this system may seem impossible to do. And yes, immediately, for most people it is. But it also isn't feasible to begin any sport, dance, or yoga like an expert. You need to learn a new skill one small step at a time. As long as you have patience for your partner and yourself, you will find satisfaction in merely trying to move the environment between you and your loved one toward increasing closeness.

Intimate listening requires that you allow yourself to be vulnerable within your relationships. Too often, people confuse weakness with vulnerability because at first glance, both emotions feel the same. The defenses you created as a child to deny and hide your pain can make it difficult to take this step. However, deciding to be exposed with a loved one by sincerely connecting through intimate listening not only enhances your mutual understanding; it also allows authentic emotion to flood your life. The more sentiment you have access to, the more energy you have for problem solving and creativity, and the more empowered you feel.

This Turning Point is so crucial to lasting love that in 1997 I wrote a book about it. With an altered title, *Intimate Listening: How to Connect to the Heart and Soul of Someone You Love*, you presently can find it on iUniverse.com.

Chapter 17

INFLUENCE VERSUS CONTROL
Taking the Long View of Change

This Turning Point is at once humbling and powerful. When you consider the changes you wish for in your partner—that he would dress better, that she would be more affectionate—it becomes obvious how little intentional control you have over his or her behavior. You can beg, nag, blackmail, and sweet-talk all you want: Controlling another person is a barrier-building method for altering his conduct, no matter how maddening it may be.

But there is a deeper force for change, which, over time, can have a tenacious effect on the relationship's environment. Rather than expending energy outward in order to control, change, or "fix" someone else, the alternative tactic—influence—requires rotating our accusatory fingers 180 degrees. You become a living example of how you would like others to behave. And, while it is no sure thing, over time, the persuasive power of influence can have a much more prolonged effect.

CONTROL VERSUS CONTROLLING

Believing that your point of view is "right" or incontestable is a barrier-building stance. When you are controlling, you are saying to a loved one, *No, you are doing it wrong. Here is the right way— my way.* This denies your partner his autonomy. By dominating everyday choices such as which route to take to the movie theater or what to order at dinner ("Why don't you get the grilled chicken instead, darling?"), you not only rob another's self-determination, but you also cheat yourself out of a dynamic, adult relationship. Usually anxiety is the emotion that fuels the drive to be control- ling. Do you really want this to be the motivator that impels your relationship? Is it appealing to be married to someone who roboti- cally does your bidding? Would this make for a sexy or interesting or vibrant partnership?

An important distinction exists between the anxiety-driven controlling of someone else and taking control of a situation. There are instances when taking control means *voluntarily* giving over control for certain tasks. This gesture can be boundary building. In any relationship, one person will inevitably be better at certain chores. A mutually satisfactory division of labor is a happy out- come of creating a shared life. Finally, here's someone who finds a perverse (to you) pleasure in laundry! It is with joy you relinquish the task of cleaning clothes. The flip side of this coin is that you'll handle the refinancing documents that she finds tedious. And thus, a team is born.

The distinction between control and controlling becomes clearer when you break it down to end results. I know someone who has spent decades "training" her husband into becoming the person she thinks she would prefer. Forty years later, he is basically the same man—silent, brilliant, and provocative. She approached her marriage like a mechanic; controlling him was her main tool. Countless dinners were spent attempting to beat down the door of his quiet intransigence. Nagging and harping, she tried to force him to conform to the husband of her dreams. Not surprisingly, it didn't work. And, to his credit, it shouldn't have. The fact is, she loves him in spite of his perceived flaws. If she had succeeded in transforming him into some loquacious companion who was always mooning on about thieves stealing diamonds for her eyes, she could have lost her challenge, and who knows what might have happened to them. Even with half a century of trying, she could not force her husband to change. And that's a good thing.

THE COUNTERINTUITIVE NATURE OF INFLUENCE

The power of influence is also obvious when you view it from a marketing perspective. The reasons you are compelled to buy a certain cereal or TV are complex, although you may be hard pressed to articulate exactly why you feel good about Cocoa Puffs or Sony. Branding is influence, and its ability to sway you often occurs beneath the surface and over an extended period of time. This phenomenon is mirrored in a long-term relationship. Whether you are aware of it or not, you are continually affecting your partner.

People tend to think of influence as a change agent that involves another. But since you only have power over your own behavior, it follows that influencing your partner begins *and ends* with you. If you hope that your lover will lead a morally sound life, your best bet is to be principled yourself. If you wish he would stop being a workaholic, let yourself enjoy the hammock on a Saturday afternoon and maybe at some point he won't be so eager to head into the office. *Maybe.* There is no guarantee that you can sway an autonomous adult into becoming cleaner or more affectionate or good (just as the makers of Cocoa Puffs can't force you to buy their product).

But people—especially couples who have been together for years—do influence each other. We are social creatures and it is our nature to want to belong. Think of your parents or grandparents or aunts and uncles who over time have morphed into an amalgam of each other. You see them dressed in their identical pressed khakis, insisting on overtipping the waitress, nodding assurance to each other in complete harmony. It's sweet and dopey and you can't imagine it will ever happen to you. But, influence plus time is a powerful equation, and although you may never convince him to go to church, there are many other differences that will slowly disappear as each of you work your powers of persuasion on the other.

LUCE AND SANDRO

Luce and Sandro met as young accountants at a firm in New York City. Attracted from the start, Sandro—a shy guy—was drawn by Luce's bubbly personality and bright outlook. Luce loved his virile, burning sexuality and how safe he made her feel.

They married almost immediately, and Luce—at first intimidated by his parents' fine home—quickly became a happy student of her mother-in-law's lifestyle. Over the course of ten years, Luce put her career aside. They had three children, and she kept an immaculate house while the children attended the same private school that their father did. After fifteen years, Luce began to feel that her role as Sandro's wife was not sufficiently stimulating. In fact, she felt that her spirit was slowly dying; what happened to the hungry first-generation immigrant, that striver, the proud girl who put herself through school?

In Luce's proactive manner, she began to think about pursuing her MBA in accounting. Course packets thickened their daily mail, but she hesitated telling Sandro her dream. Luce knew a battle was on the horizon. Summoning courage, Luce joined Sandro on their back deck one spring evening after the house quieted. She used their ritual of sharing a glass of red wine at day's end to reveal her desire to go back to school.

"The kids don't need me 24/7. I really think this could be a self-esteem booster. And, besides, it would be a good example for the girls."

They sat in silence as Sandro stared out onto the darkening lawn. In the fading light, she couldn't read his expression. Finally, he said in a voice so low she had to lean in to hear, "Why would you want to do this to us? I've always said yours is a full-time job—the most important kind. Now, you want to go crunch numbers for some company rather than care for your family?"

Luce was furious at his comment, which made her feel guilty. His attempt to control his wife's pursuits erected a barrier between them that would become damaging over time.

LUCE PURSUES HER DREAM

Five years after that tense conversation, Luce had earned her MBA and was two years into her private practice. The women in her community had spread the word about Luce's talents and energy; she had more business than she could handle. Happiness in her professional life, however, was directly disproportionate to her home environment. Sandro had become hypercritical and controlling about everything from the cleaning to how crisp his vegetables were cooked. How could Luce and Sandro resolve this issue and rediscover their original passion? The challenge here is to uncover what lies beneath their distress so that each can genuinely feel concern for what is bothering the other while discovering what is important for themselves.

For Luce, part of her was tempted to give up her accounting practice entirely. In those dark moments, she determined that the work was not worth losing her marriage. The problem with this non-solution is that by returning to her more limiting role, Luce would not be going back in time. She would still be a woman who felt she had already lived those wonderful, exhausting days of babies and toddlers. That time was over; Luce was claustrophobic at even the thought of staying home all day.

Luce spent time allowing Sandro to explain what was upsetting him, in order to truly understand where Sandro's anxiety about her role as a working mom was coming from. To do this, she had only to look across town to his parents, who not only adhered to strict gender roles for themselves, but also expected their only son to follow suit. His mother's ability to stay home was—to Sandro's family—a status symbol that showcased their prosperity. This upbringing clashed with Luce's determination to work, arousing perplexed feelings in Sandro. Was he not good enough to support his wife? What would people think? All of these questions lurked beneath the surface as Sandro lashed out in confusion and helplessness.

By understanding how Sandro's upbringing had influenced his views on gender roles, Luce could then work to build a bridge back to her husband without losing herself in the process. Knowing she had only the power to alter her own behavior, Luce conducted an experiment: She told herself that for one month, she would completely ignore his criticisms, and, instead of acting angry and cold in the face of his venom, she would be sweet, soft, and supportive. Could this influence Sandro to do the same?

At first, Luce had a difficult time not rising to his bait if he complained about household neglect. After a few weeks, however, she found that her refusal to fight began to neutralize his attacks. She was breaking a pattern of behavior that had gone on for years. Sandro—also unhappy with their situation—was caught off guard by her kindness and began to feel that a wall between them was cracking.

It was slowly dawning on Sandro that his wife's love of life had been the draw that originally caused him to fall in love with her. Each time his criticism was ignored, it was as if his rudeness bounced back and stuck to him, hurting Sandro more than it hurt

Luce. The sweeter she was, the more ridiculous he felt for putting up such a fight over the dust or the overcooked food. Several months later, for her birthday, Sandro bought his wife a beautiful green leather briefcase, signifying for both of them a fresh beginning.

The choice to either influence or control a loved one greatly alters the environment between two people. Imagine your intimate relationship is like a solar system, with each extraterrestrial body influencing the other. Exerting this subtle push and pull keeps you in each other's orbit, harmoniously circling. Controlling, on the other hand, is jarring, and sets both of you out of the natural trajectory of your relationship, which is based on each partner's innate nature. Raising your consciousness so that you are aware of when you choose to either control or influence your partner increases the opportunity to make your relationship work.

Chapter 18

CONSTRUCTIVE CRITICISM VERSUS DESTRUCTIVE CRITICISM

Learning to Give Compassionate Feedback

Critiquing a loved one is like traversing a tightrope high above the ground. One misstep—a harsh look or word, an exaggeration—and you fall into an abyss of misunderstanding, blame, and hurt. The choice between constructive and destructive criticism is especially challenging because it is often in a moment of stress that you are tempted to voice the changes you wish to see in your partner.

A CRITICAL DISTINCTION

"You always have to be the center of attention!" or "You never get up with the baby!" are charges that may feel true after the interminable dinner party or latest sleepless night. In actuality you are categorizing your partner and putting him in a box. But the relief of lashing out in blaming anger is short-lived. More to the point, this type of finger-pointing will not further positive change within your partner. Rather, it is *destructive*, causing a barrier to slam down between you and your lover as he quickly feels unseen and unappreciated. He then becomes defensive and matches your anger with his own, "Oh, yeah!? Well, you never . . . ." This is a scenario in which no one learns, and no one grows. Love cowers in the corner, waiting out the storm.

Destructive criticism arises from a desire for the other to change, ignited by such feelings as anxiety, anger, or—ironically— self-criticism. On the other hand, constructive criticism is an opportunity to be attentive to both your own and your partner's needs and motivations. Pause and take a thoughtful moment to ask yourself, *Why does it really bother me that he gets all the laughs at the party?* or *I wonder if he still feels nervous that he'll drop our newborn?* The more tuned in you are toward yourself and the other person, the more your criticism will be received as a helpful suggestion and not an attempt to tear down and destroy.

THE FOUR BARRIERS OF DESTRUCTIVE CRITICISM

Many of my patients have difficulty successfully negotiating this Turning Point. Instead, they tend to fall into one of four extremes.

First, there are two extremes for those who are on the giving side of criticism:

1. The first group is fearful of offering any feedback because of resistance to incurring anger. Although they may have a legitimate reason to criticize, their fear of conflict mutes

their voice of concern. This can lead to a lifetime of quiet frustration, inhibiting mutual growth.

2. The second group comprises those who are overly disapproving. Addicted to being right, they rarely fail to voice their opinion about their partners' missteps, no matter how insignificant. But unsolicited feedback, especially if it is unintentionally or intentionally meant to evoke shame, can easily be regarded as a boundary violation. Shame is a feeling that there is something wrong within us that cannot be changed. Over time, shaming breaks down self-trust as well as the trust of another. The recipient of the ceaseless "advice" either begins to hide his or her true self to avoid attack, or leaves for good.

For those standing in critique's spotlight, there are also barrier-building extremes:

1. The first group includes those who welcome any and all criticism, adopting their loved one's feedback without pause. All reactions toward you contain hidden information about the giver, so in order to wisely apply—or reject—the pointers your partner offers you, you need to embark upon an internal dialogue that asks the following questions: *Why is he telling me this (at this moment)? What does it tell me about my partner? When I consider his feedback honestly and without defenses, does he perhaps have a point?* After answering these questions, you can then decide how—and if—the criticism can improve who you are.

2. The second group on the receiving end of criticism includes those who are narcissistically injured (deeply insulted) by any censure. If you are crying in the bathroom because your lover reminded you of your tendency to tailgate, you

not only discourage constructive criticism, but also choose obliviousness over growth.

These barrier-building behaviors make up the body of the beast we call destructive criticism. For some of us, the manner in which you give or receive criticism was learned at the knee of an overly critical parent or—equally as damaging—a mom or dad who was exceedingly permissive. Both extremes in parenting produce individuals who are behind the learning curve on this Turning Point and must unlearn these ingrained obstacles. It's worth the effort. If you can't give or take feedback well, you stymie one of the by-products of a long-term relationship: that you are able to serve as witnesses for each other, which can in turn help you to become your best self.

HARRIS AND MADELINE

For Harris, a boisterous thirty-year-old actor, being open to giving and receiving criticism comes naturally. He loves everything about his new girlfriend, Madeline . . . well, almost everything. She has a habit of arriving at his performances after the curtain is up. Not only that, she often appears at the bar where he works hours after she promised she would. Walking in the park one afternoon, Harris voiced his frustration with Madeline's lateness, but after an earnest apology, she became withdrawn. Noting her quiet mood, he said, "It's not that big of a deal. We should be able to say when certain things bother us and not have the other completely shut down."

Sensing she had taken this as yet another criticism, he adopted a new tactic: "Okay—let's make it even. What is it about me that you absolutely can't stand?" He stopped in front of her, forcing her to look into his smiling eyes. "There's gotta be something—the way I chew, how I dress, my hatred of the opera . . . ."

Finally, Madeline broke out in laughter, but said, "I don't know what you want from me, Harris. You're perfect. I have no complaints."

Harris was irritated. Her flattering comment struck him more as evasion than praise. "I feel like you're hiding from me when you do that," he said.

They walked a bit farther and sat on a bench. "Jodi and I were talking about guys with glasses the other day," she said, seemingly changing the subject. "She said she's not into them, but I disagreed, because after sex I can get out of bed and they can't see me clearly."

Harris, with his 20/20 vision, waited to see where she was going with this. "You see, I have so much self-criticism, Harris, that I am afraid if I told you something bothers me, you would reciprocate. I have a hard time taking criticism. To me, it's all destructive. From you, it feels devastating."

Admitting this was a positive step for Madeline. Growing up, her parents gave her only exaggerated positive feedback. Whatever she got on her report card was "exceptional"; the boys she brought home reeking of cheap booze were "in love with her." She didn't have a curfew because her "judgment was impeccable." Now, as an adult, she has no real concept of how her actions, including her tardiness, affected other people. Madeline must make her way in a world full of critical people who expect an honest give-and-take.

When a new relationship begins, like Harris and Madeline's, giving—and receiving—constructive criticism is part of the process of discovery. However, it can be especially challenging at this tender stage to offer your reaction. *What if he doesn't take it well? What if she leaves me?* It can seem easier, especially for a novice like Madeline, to just let things go and hope for the best. However, mutual feedback is crucial for love to flourish.

BREAK IT TO ME GENTLY

Constructive criticism means offering a mirror to a loved one that will help her move toward her edge of growth, toward her best self. Recall Auderseu's fable of the naked emperor parading down the street. All of his lackeys are afraid to tell him that the new suit he just purchased from a swindler is nonexistent. As he proudly waves to the people, a child shouts out, "The emperor is naked!" Did the emperor need this feedback? Do you imagine there are times when you are metaphorically naked and no one is telling you? Who better to point out that you have spinach in your teeth or have inadvertently hurt someone's feelings than the person closest to you, the one you trust the most? Conversely, wouldn't it be unkind to stay mute as your lover proudly sports an unflattering (to your eyes) Fu Manchu mustache?

So, what is the best method for offering criticism that is well received? Here are the three steps for achieving constructive feedback:

1. Begin the conversation with an "I," rather than a "you," statement. This defuses feelings of defensiveness in the listener and lessens the finger-pointing factor. Authors Rhoda Baruch, Edith Grotberg, and Suzanne Stutman offer a wonderfully specific strategy in their book, *Creative Anger: Putting That Powerful Emotion to Good Use.* They suggest framing a critical statement in this way: "I feel ___ when ___ because___." By using this script as a starting point for a difficult conversation, you offer your partner the opportunity to become aware of your hidden fears and other emotions. For example, "I feel embarrassed when you are curt with my friends because my parents never allowed my friends to hang out when I was in high school. I was ashamed of my parents' inhospitality."

2. Give your partner some positive reinforcement. No matter how serious your critique, your loved one still

has many of the fantastic qualities you fell for way back when. For example, you could mention that although you wish he were nicer to your friends, you *do* appreciate his being so warm to your parents, especially since they are difficult people. This tells him that you notice the good in him as well, and keeps the door open for mutual understanding. A variation on positive reinforcement accompanying constructive criticism is to tell your partner that one of his special qualities has a dark side to it. For example, "You are honest and this makes me happy that I can trust your word, but when it comes to friends you are *brutally* honest and it can hurt their feelings."

3. Ask for help. Most people respond well to a call to action, especially when the person requesting it is a loved one. Instead of hearing, "This is what you do that bothers me—now go change," which can leave him reeling with no firm direction, he hears, "This is how your actions affect me. Do you have any thoughts about how I could let it go?" A cry for help may enhance his feelings of empathy, once again subverting a reflexive need to be defensive.

Now that you are familiar with the key steps of giving constructive criticism, imagine the following conversation:

You: "I feel frustrated when you are unsociable to my friends because I become embarrassed."

Him: "It's not that I don't like them; we just have nothing in common."

You: "Really? How come you see it that way?"

Him: "Your friends seem snobby. I feel uncomfortable when they talk about money because my father was a truck driver. I'm polite enough."

You: "Wow, I am so sorry you feel that way. But now I understand your vastly different response to them than to almost anyone else, including my parents, to whom you are so generous. Tricia's barbecue is on Sunday. Do you think we could make a fresh start?"

Him: "I'll try."

Your closing statement implies this will be a team effort and you will be more sensitive to his self-consciousness without personalizing it. On Sunday, when he steps away from the comfort of the men surrounding the grill to talk to the hostess, you can smile to yourself knowing that he understands you are on his side.

Another important element of constructive criticism is maintaining your sense of humor. Self-seriousness is the enemy of successfully giving and accepting feedback. Let's face it: Each of us is fumbling through life, making mistakes despite our best intentions. If you keep your flawed humanity in mind, and are able to laugh at yourself, it can lessen the sting of criticism. Rather than responding to feedback with grumbles of self-recrimination, defensiveness, and anger, humor pulls the lever that switches your emotional train onto a different track.

Suppose your partner says it drives him crazy that you tend to bring up inflammatory topics in social settings. Which of the following is the happier scenario? You can get mad, deny it, or vociferously defend your right to stimulate conversation, bridging no gap between your two perspectives. Or, you can choose to laugh it off, saying, "Oh, yeah? Good thing you said something; I was just about to ask for the mail lady's stance on abortion." As you both chuckle, you can take that moment to pause and consider what your loved one is trying to convey. In such a breather, you have an opportunity to thoughtfully read between the lines as to what his request is all about. When you do this, it will influence your next move and help you to move toward the same page as your significant other.

The distinction between constructive and destructive criticism rests on a willingness to tune in first to yourself and then to your loved one's motivations, rather than carelessly stating your case, emotional blinders intact. This Turning Point is especially important because it sustains your relationship on two levels. The first is intimate knowledge—it helps you to better know yourself as well as your lover. The second is power in the world—it supports your significant other by affirming his strengths while finding a way to serve as a mirror to his growth, those areas of his behavior that he may be unaware are creating obstacles.

Remember: Keep your sense of humor within easy reach! Nothing dissipates a tense moment like laughter.

Part III
Personal Power

Chapter 19

DECIDING VERSUS CRAVING
Deciding What Is and What Isn't
Worth Having

The word *crave* sounds as powerful as it is. So phonetically close to *slave*, it connotes a force that can indeed capture (and enrapture) our thoughts and bodies. To have a craving, to give *in* to a craving, can be so utterly satisfying that some people would drive through the night, pay too much, risk it all, to get what they long for—whether it's a person, a smoke, or a hot fudge sundae. There is something rather glamorous about surrendering to a craving, something decadent, and popular culture does nothing to sway us from our desires. Sex and food, alcohol and cigarettes: Those clever marketers know what they are doing.

A QUESTION OF EXTREMES

In truth, although you may crave things that are unhealthy for you, you can also yearn for a bit of sunshine, the feel of the sand between your toes, or—as anyone who has ever been pregnant knows—a variety of foods, both nutritious and not. Giving in to a craving is subjective, a behavior that can have negative or positive repercussions for you and your loved one.

Unlike craving, deciding means consciously choosing how you wish to spend your time or what you consume. Whereas craving has a built-in inertia that pulls you toward your desire, deciding says, "Now, wait just a minute!" Weighing the options, you analyze and take your time. *If I eat this sundae, I have to spend an extra hour at the gym. Is it worth it? Should I just have the rice cake?* Making smart decisions, rather than giving in to impulse, can save you and loved ones from pain down the line. If your choice is to either call a cab or get behind the wheel—or into bed with a stranger—after one too many drinks, weighing which option is smarter is time well-invested. Often, if you know you are going to be in a situation where a craving is likely to be triggered, it is better to make the choice of what would be a winning outcome before the event begins. In this case, that might be enlisting a friend to promise to take you home—alone.

Of course, excessively intellectualizing a decision can take the spice out of life. If you are so busy weighing and measuring whether or not to seize a chance to get what you truly want, you risk becoming frozen with indecision. Overthinking your desires is stultifying and robs you of those spontaneous moments that you look back on happily, that crazy road trip or love affair that leaves you shaking your head in wonder at the adventure of living. It is a question of extremes.

THE REPERCUSSIONS OF CRAVING

How does craving affect an intimate relationship? Isn't it my business alone if I eat the box of cookies or spend the afternoon watching porn on the Internet? Well, no. The very nature of a loving relationship is that your actions affect your partner. Obsessively giving in to your yearnings can build barriers between yourself and a loved one if it isolates him, puts you or him at risk, or violates his trust.

In our increasingly electronic society, a common hunger is spending hours zoned out in front of the computer or television. There are literally endless opportunities for entertainment—how amazing! Or is it? If one partner has little interest in prolonged screen time and the other can't resist, the former may eventually feel isolated. The other option is to decide—and express—how much TV viewing you plan on enjoying. You could say, "Honey, I'm going to watch this *Seinfeld* rerun to unwind after a tough day." At this point, you can invite her to join you, or not, claiming you need half an hour alone. This is an explicit boundary that lets both partners know what to expect.

Some people desire the exact opposite of planning, instead thriving on excitement, spontaneity, gambling, the unexpected, life against all odds. Suppose you are someone who craves not the cigarette, but the risk of smoking. You may be aware that the odds are against you, but still yearn for the thrill of the slots. This can lead to a life full of surprises, and can be tough on your partner if it isn't in his or her nature to push the limits. When you put your health or financial well-being at risk, your loved one is helpless, on the outside looking in, while you impulsively indulge.

A mundane, but common, example of this is the difficulty many couples have when catching a plane. The person who craves excitement prefers to wait until the last minute to head out to the airport. He feels there is ample time; he rolls his eyes at his more cautious counterpart. "If we leave now, we're going to be sitting at the airport bar for over an hour—mark my words." The other half of the couple, who hates the stress of possibly missing the plane, will park herself by the door, anxiety rising, as the minutes tick by. This safety-mismatched couple yearns for two different things: risk and security. Without their deciding to meet in the middle, this issue will forever be problematic.

Succumbing to a craving is at its most damaging when substance abuse is involved. If one or both partners have an addiction, the risk to body, mind, and spirit is real. Addiction takes away personal power; the option to decide goes out the window. At its worst, it supercedes devotion to anything else—family, career, spouse. In order to defeat this craving, the first step is acknowledging the problem. Opening your eyes to the damage you are inflicting on your loved ones can be a painful awakening, but with their support and a commitment to the appropriate twelve-step program, or other therapeutic interventions, there can be healing.

JUSTIN AND KATHERINE

Justin met Katherine at a party in Malibu when they were both in their early twenties. They had come out to Hollywood to try to make their mark—he as a screenwriter, she as an actress. Their relationship was intense. Most nights, they stayed up until dawn, with the help of mountains of their friends' cocaine.

Five years later, Katherine was pregnant and feeling the urge to nest. They decided to move back east to New Jersey to be close to family. For most of their adult lives, the couple had spent their evenings drunk or getting high—often both. Now, Katherine felt that trading in illicit drugs for prenatal vitamins was the right thing to do. Justin agreed, up to a point. He often traveled back to LA for business meetings or bachelor parties, where it was the same old scene: The evening would begin with cocktails, and keep right on going with coke. He would tell Katherine—and himself—that he would only have a couple of drinks and call it a night. Inevitably, Katherine would call his hotel at two or three in the morning and there would be no answer.

One such morning, she picked up the phone to his groggy, pre-coffee voice: "Hey, babe. Sorry . . . late night with Larry and those guys."

"Yeah, sounds like you had a good time. Listen, I hate to be a bitch, but come on—we made a deal."

"I know. It's just that one thing led to another. I only took a couple bumps. I swear, this is the last time."

"I've heard that before. Come on, you're about to be a father. If I can stay sober for nine months, you can at least make an effort to lay off the coke." She hung up before he could reply.

The funny thing is, Katherine knew he regretted it. She could hear it in his voice. Still, she couldn't resist being judgmental. After all, they were going to raise a child together. Could she depend on him? For Justin, her reaction deepened his shame at giving in to his desire for coke, which helped give him courage in social settings. He considered just not admitting it next time, the thought of which only sharpened his self-hatred.

USING TEAMWORK TO KEEP CRAVING AT BAY

How can this couple best handle their desire—both past and present—for cocaine? The key is for them to form a united front, which will necessitate honesty on both of their parts. Katherine has to own up to the discomfort behind her judgment. Presently she is pregnant and in a way the fetus is acting as a police officer. As long as he is in her uterus Katherine is safe from temptation. She has to acknowledge to her husband that she judges him in order to hide the fear that once she is no longer pregnant she also will be tempted.

Justin must acknowledge that when Katherine judges him it makes him feel even worse about his powerlessness over his cravings. The more she can support him and perhaps agree to go to a twelve-step program with him, the sooner they will find a solid way to be a team. If Justin and Katherine can consent to a mutual point of view about substance abuse, their team will be better at withstanding the pressure of the outside world. They both will need to own the reality that they are essentially powerless over cocaine and that they can challenge themselves to hold on to their sobriety one day at a time. Becoming overly confident that they are beyond temptation is the beginning of self-delusion and the path away from jointly protecting each other and the boundaries around their emerging family. Accepting that cocaine is a scourge that their family will have to acknowledge for the rest of their days is the best strategy for keeping this craving at bay. The more there is a disagreement between them over this subject, the more barriers will be erected, which over time could put them both at risk.

MODERATION IS THE KEY

You know you have given in to a badly chosen craving if, like Justin, you are left with a feeling of emptiness and hollowness, or at least regret. The fact is, some of the things for which you pine are a substitution for something else that is missing in your life. As we all know, brownies don't hug you back, and booze won't disguise your insecurities for long. Solving these problems takes hard emotional weightlifting. On the other hand, you know you are standing on safe ground if, after indulging, you feel joyful, fulfilled, like you just gave yourself a well-earned present. In this instance, you were actually deciding to succumb to a passion, whether it is lovemaking during baby's naptime, a ninety-minute Swedish massage, a day alone at the beach, or a hot fudge sundae.

The key to becoming strong within your relationship and yourself is moderation—of both your passions and your more rational side. There is nothing wrong with indulging in what you desire, if it does not cause physical or emotional harm. As well, it can add to the intensity of your existence if you make choices that conform with your value system. For example, if I indulge in gambling, what does this say about my value system? Will slot machines support my path to living a purposeful life? Are they fulfilling? For some people whom I know and love, slot machines bring joy, excitement, and escape. The machines do no harm to others and provide some stimulating excitement. These people can say yes, they match my overall value system and add to my life's purpose to be available for fun as well as work.

The more you are in sync with your partner, the less likely barriers will emerge—even when one of you gives in to a momentary urge. Unremitting craving is a barrier because you are not choosing; you are submitting. It becomes a negative force when one person is an outsider to the other person's cravings, or when both couples are joined in excessively succumbing to a mutual longing.

To decide whether you are indulging in a passion or succumbing to a craving, note the ensuing emotion. Feeling contented after the experience would put it in the "passion" category. Feeling empty and ashamed is the "powerless over my cravings" category. Looking for a balanced existence supports a couple continuing to flourish in their lives together. This equilibrium will allow you to enjoy life's pleasures while at the same time making the wise decisions that create stability and long-term contentment.

Chapter 20

FIGHTING FAIR VERSUS FIGHTING UNFAIR
Defining a Fair Fight

Like companionship and intimacy, fighting is part of the package when you embark on a long-term relationship. And, as much as it brings to mind conflict, fighting can actually be a force for good—clearing the air, bridging misunderstandings, and ultimately bringing you closer together. Without ever engaging in arguments, you run the risk of becoming invisible. While you silently swallow your complaints, desires, and need for change, your partner skips along happily, unaware of your dissatisfaction. Fair fighting is the fresh breeze that blows away the smog of your discontent.

THE LOW ROAD

That fresh breeze turns corrosive if you choose to fight unfairly, however. Your sense of justice was well honed way before falling in love. Back on the playground, you learned what was fair game and what was hitting below the belt. "Hey—that's not fair!" the smaller kid cries as his tormenters taunt him for his stature, shaming him by taking his hat and running away. It stings because he is helpless to change the stubborn fact that he is smaller. There is no way to win.

As adults, this phenomenon persists. In a moment of anger, it is easy to take the low road, to lash out at a partner's weak points. The irony is that it is the very fact of our intimacy that makes us vulnerable to attack. Who knows your sensitivities better than your lover? Baring your belly in trust, you can't imagine that the midnight confession about your dad's affair or the part of your body you hate could be used against you down the road. So, when he *goes there* during a fight, his words can feel like a punch to the gut.

Here's how to define the difference between fair and unfair fighting when it comes to a love relationship: The trick to fair fighting is to express yourself during conflict so the other person hears your need while keeping the playing field even. Contrast that idea against the following list, which depicts the six moves in unfair fighting meant to induce powerlessness in your opponent.

1. **Shaming:** Criticizing something that can't be changed or was revealed to you in a moment of vulnerability.
2. **Blackmail:** Intimidating by exposure if your partner doesn't do your bidding.
3. **Threatening:** Promising to do something hurtful if your partner doesn't do your bidding.
4. **The Past:** Bringing up unresolved fights or historical hurts.

5. **Bringing in a Third Party:** Conjuring up the opinion of family or mutual friends who supposedly agree with you on the matter at hand.

6. **Withholding:** Keeping your feelings a secret by not talking.

The couple in the following story are experts at unfair fighting.

SHARI AND RONNIE

Ronnie spends half his time in New York with his wife, Shari, and the other half battling his debts at the tables in Atlantic City. Their problems began when Ronnie asked Shari to open a checking account in her name for his use (if he had an account in his name, creditors could obtain the money). It didn't take long before the bank began calling Shari about "her" frequently overdrawn account, which was blackening her perfect credit score.

Hearing Ronnie's key in the lock, Shari began her diatribe: "I got another warning from the bank today. I think you need to work on your resume rather than your blackjack skills."

"Welcome home, dear," Ronnie said sarcastically. "Jesus! You are turning into a narcoleptic nag, just like your mother."

"I think you mean *narcissistic*, fool. This is what I get for marrying someone with six months of community college under his belt. Why didn't you stay in Jersey with all the other trash?"

SHAMING THOSE WE LOVE

Unfair fighting is one of the most corrosive human behaviors you can participate in, especially when it comes to humiliating a person close to you. Shaming means finding fault with something he cannot change. You are saying that a part of him is unacceptable—which means, in essence, that he is unacceptable. There are three common pitfalls to watch out for, as they quickly lead to unfair fighting.

AVOID MENTIONING FAMILY

The first pitfall is speaking with disdain about your partner's parents, siblings, or other relatives. Imagine listening quietly as your lover complains that his mother is vicious, or neglectful, or just plain annoying. He's really getting revved up, recalling all of her faults, when you step in with a story of your own: "And remember that time she actually hung up on me because of who I was voting for? What an idiot!" What was expressed in commiseration quickly falls flat as he steps in to defend her: "Well, consider how she grew up!"

Picking up the theme of his awful mother is hurtful. Your husband's mother is his original love object. He is attached to her forever. During an argument, this becomes even more fraught and can lead to an unfair fight. Yelling, "You're just like your mother!" or "No wonder you and your sister can't get it together," shines a harsh light on a loved one's place of origin, something over which he has no control. The feelings of shame this engenders will override constructive dialogue as anger takes the reins.

AVOID MENTIONING SEXUAL PERFORMANCE

A second area where shaming can cause damage is sexual performance. Criticizing your lover's sexuality or physical attributes with a malice-tinged voice can cause a permanent freeze both in the bedroom and out. When this attack happens during a sexual encounter ("You're quicker than a thirteen-year-old boy!"), you are teaching your lover that sex with you can be embarrassing and is something to avoid. Equally damaging is an insult during a seemingly unrelated argument: "The last thing we need is a big SUV. *God*, get over your small penis already!"

Showing impatience with a loved one's sexuality will impede carnal satisfaction. So, how do you address this sensitive topic when you long for change in the bedroom? When it comes to sex, it is up to the person who wants it to find the path to it. Choose action over insults by initiating lovemaking with mutual pleasure as the goal through trial and error, encouragement, and playful hints. For some couples that I know, finding sexual pleasure requires imagination, kindness, and a willingness to take risks and step out of the tried and true.

AVOID MENTIONING FAILURES

The third area where many succumb to unfair fighting is achievement—or the lack thereof. If you are disappointed that your partner is underfunctioning compared to what he is capable of, don't keep this thought solely to yourself (see Chapter 18, Constructive Criticism versus Destructive Criticism). Simply lashing out, however, could call to mind the insecurities your partner may be harboring about his intelligence, charisma, or ambition. We all perform at our best when we feel confident and have a trustworthy support system. Conversely, when you hear, "You lazy idiot!" or "Some mother you are!" it could reinforce a belief in your own worthlessness and trigger even greater retreat.

FAIR FIGHTING IS NOT EASY

The choice to fight fairly rather than impulsively lashing out can be challenging. Recall some of your more heated arguments. You know exactly what to say to cut your partner down a notch. Few of us are immune to the feelings of powerlessness that compel us to fight unfairly. When angry words are parried back and forth, you may say, "I'm just reacting to the awful thing he said." You sharpen your claws and fight back with equally harsh words, hoping to somehow "win." This is a child's logic of who-hit-who-first. "You say my mother's an alcoholic slob? Well, then, let's talk about your creepy dad hitting on my maid of honor!" There is no way to come out a winner here—it is a mirage. You are mimicking destructive behavior. Why follow him down such a low road?

FINDING A WAY OUT

Rather than lashing out in equal measure, there are several steps that can keep you on the high road, acting heroically. Learning how to fight fairly, although difficult, is a laudable interpersonal skill. It allows you to maintain personal power with calm integrity during even the harshest conflicts.

Imagine your lover has made an unfair crack about your struggle with your weight. Following are the six steps to engaging in this fight fairly:

1. Resist personalizing this low blow. Her comment reflects her feelings of powerlessness and possibly reveals her own body image discomfort.

2. Detach by engaging in a separate activity apart from your lover. Say, "You are making me angry. I can't speak to you right now because I'm afraid I'll say something I don't mean."

3. While apart, consider her point of view. What is she trying to convey? Worries about your health? Her own health? Or something else entirely? Did she lash out to hurt you or get your attention? Put yourself in her shoes; you may gain insight.

4. After an interval has passed, choose a moment to reintroduce the subject. The helpful construct we learned in Chapter 18 ("I feel ___ when ___ because___") is a good opener. You could say, "I felt hurt when you called me fat because I was heavy as a kid and have struggled with it my entire life."

5. At this point, she may elaborate on what is bothering her. (Perhaps she recalls her overweight dad dying of a heart attack at a young age.) A question such as, "What can we do to move forward?" reinforces the fact that you are a team. Own the problem and offer concrete, constructive solutions. A joint gym membership? A commitment to cutting out junk food? Working toward the same goal—

especially one that caused the conflict—confers a feeling of closeness.

6. Keep in mind: Not all conflict is resolvable. She may insist she had always hoped for a thinner man. But perhaps her fantasy 160-pounder would not be as funny or good in bed or generous as you, which you can remind her of as you charm her into smiling. The real heroism in fighting fair is knowing your own value, rather than being buffeted to and fro by shaming comments.

SHARI AND RONNIE REVISITED

An interesting thing happened when Shari and Ronnie came into my office one afternoon. I asked Shari why she stayed with Ronnie, given their frequent and painful fighting. She paused, thought for a long while, and then said that he makes a delicious homemade pizza. In that moment, I felt little hope for this couple's long-term happiness. But then, just as I was privately succumbing to my own reverie of defeat, they looked at each other and began laughing. I joined them and we spent what seemed like several minutes just releasing the tension until tears ran down our cheeks.

It soon came out that the look they had given each other was a private joke that meant, "What are we doing here when we could be somewhere else having sex?" They both saw the irony of sitting in a therapist's office complaining about each other while life outside could have so much beauty in it. It was a magical moment.

Shari and Ronnie teach us a wonderful lesson about the lifelines love can throw our way even during its most difficult moments. Humor and sexual energy can short-circuit a thorny argument, paving the way for kinder, more constructive dialogue. If you can access it, a moment such as Shari and Ronnie's reminds us how easy it is to get caught up in the banality of life's annoyances, forgetting how fortunate we are to have love in our lives.

Fighting fair becomes an easier choice the older you become. In your twenties and thirties, you are still defining who you are. The insecurity that comes along with such growth means it can be difficult not to take things personally. With experience, you realize that harsh words spoken in anger have everything to do with the speaker and little to do with you. But, even if you're twenty-five and just at the beginning of your journey, you can still avoid another decade of unfair fights. After all, this book is a tool to help you gain received wisdom without having to go through more hard knocks than are absolutely necessary.

Chapter 21

SUPPORT VERSUS PROTECTION
Establishing an Empowering Stance

When you were a child, it was your parents' job to both support and protect you. Ideally, they cheered you on from the bleachers, sustaining your youthful endeavors. On the way home, they made sure you were buckled in and carefully bandaged your cuts and scrapes. In this model scenario, you felt safe, secure in the knowledge that you could do anything. In a loving adult relationship, can't you simply carry on this legacy?

COMMON MISPERCEPTIONS

Actually, the perceived difference between support and protection becomes more distinct as you mature, because not everyone experienced a satisfying dose of encouragement and security as children. Having developed habitual reactions to caregivers who fell somewhere along the continuum between overprotective and neglectful, your grown-up self may have a less than ideal understanding of support—both how to give and receive it. This can create confusion in understanding each other's intentions.

For example, imagine you meet someone at a party who could be a good professional contact for your husband. You mean to be supportive when you tell this person your husband is looking for work. Relaying the encounter later at home, you may be mystified that he sees you as protectively meddling in his affairs. "I don't need you out there as my headhunter," he says, embarrassed at being publicly outed as jobless. Having grown up with distracted parents, he experiences your protection as demeaning.

Such misunderstandings lay fertile ground for barriers, obstacles to long-term love. Both the choice to support and that to protect can have unintended repercussions. Supporting means standing beside someone you love and giving whatever it is he or she needs to flourish. Ferreting out these needs over time, through trial and error, leads to consistent sustenance, which builds trust.

Being protective, on the other hand, can result from projecting onto someone you love what you wish you had experienced as a child. If you are overprotective of your partner, you may have felt unsheltered when young. Your parents may have been busy working, raising other siblings, or distracted by each other, either by seemingly loving closeness or by their ugly battles. The result: Rather than respecting a loved one's boundaries, you charge forth, hoping to be a white (or bronze or dark) knight. This could have everything to do with your own unexpressed needs and little to do with your partner's.

WHY PROTECTION CAN EQUAL CONTROL

Whereas support is collaborative, providing an emotional trampoline to sustain your partner's efforts, protection is hierarchical, with the person offering it regarding the other as weaker. The idea of being defended has certainly changed. Now that we are no longer in the cave and there is no need to fend off Stone Age beasts, males have few occasions to physically shield their partners, except perhaps in the case of mugging or other acts of criminal aggression. If you need protection and receive it, you feel happy. (Who would discourage heroism?)

More often, however, protecting someone "for his or her own good" is perceived as control. The husband who drops his wife off right outside her office each day insists he's defending her from "the maniacs on the road." Why would such an outwardly generous act go unappreciated? Because protecting an adult without consent unintentionally implies that the other is lacking sufficient personal power. Disregarding our partner's autonomy, we mask a desire to control an anxiety-provoking situation (at least for us) with the seemingly noble wish to protect.

CHARLES AND EDITH

Charles laughingly called himself a "benevolent despot." Like kings of old who were their people's rulers and protectors, he insisted his wife, Edith, not drive when he is in the car, not work outside the home, and remain uninvolved in their finances. And if a boy picked on one of his daughters at school, you can bet he'd show up on the playground the next day to scare the pants off the kid. The result of all this "benevolence" was a wife who outwardly went along with it yet was inwardly frustrated by feelings of helplessness, and children who learned to keep their problems to themselves.

Charles felt that he was doing the right thing. When he was a child, he had no one on his side to protect him from his older cousin, who molested him under the table while discussing the latest NBA standings with Charles's dad. The humiliation of being abused in his father's presence left him feeling utterly powerless. Five years younger than his twin brothers, they further isolated him by teasing him sexually with girls they brought into their shared bedroom. He pretended to be sleeping while the girls undressed, but still feels like a voyeur who watched them through half-closed eyes.

Charles vowed that his family would not experience this kind of neglect. His concern for his wife (and kids) was based on love, but they were often fearful of him. A true patriarch, he never allowed Edith the freedom to make her own decisions or her own mistakes, which caused barriers between them. She felt his dominance as control. A shy, ambitious woman, she burned with an inner fire that threatened to explode the longer she stayed "safe" at home.

What are the signs to look for in a loved one if you suspect you are overprotective? If your loved one is exhibiting behaviors such as helplessness, withdrawal, rebelliousness, anger, and/or cutting you off, ask yourself, "Am I overly vigilant?" If you suspect the answer is yes, back off. There is nothing to lose by doing less if you question whether you are overdoing.

CHARLES BACKS OFF

As Charles slowly came to this realization through therapy, Edith was able to carve out some independence. A turning point occurred when she decided to rent a painting studio with a friend. To their annoyance, the landlord had failed to keep his promise of adding burglarproof locks. Edith dreaded telling Charles about this snag, fearing he would overreact. She was right. Charles first threatened to go "have a little talk" with the landlord. Then, still fuming, he said, "I'll just pay for the damn locks myself!"

"You can't save me from every little obstacle that comes up," Edith pleaded. "Just let me handle this myself."

Charles took a hard look at his reaction. He noticed that he was disproportionately (compared to Edith) agitated by the landlord's inaction. His wife didn't seem upset. He considered that perhaps the problem was his. Could it be that his irritation was residual anger at his dad? Was his defense of his wife actually an incarnation of love for the boy still living inside of him? Once he reflected on this possibility, he saw that he had a choice: to be protective or supportive.

In what way could Charles act supportively in this situation? Rooted in understanding another's limitation, the first step would be to ask Edith if she needed help. This is a crucial starting point in recognizing where her boundaries lie. If she says, "Actually, if the landlord doesn't get the locks in by Friday, could you call?" Charles knows that making the phone call will not be overstepping her boundaries. Or, she may say that she will handle it, in which case the only acceptable action is to let go.

CHOOSING TO BE SUPPORTIVE

Mutual support is one of the benefits of a lifelong love. British psychiatrist John Bowlby, a leader in the study of attachment theory, in his seminal work *Separation: Anxiety and Anger, Attachment and Loss* writes: "Human beings of all ages are found to be at their happiest and to be able to deploy their talents to best advantage when they are confident that standing behind them, there are one or more trusted persons who will come to their aid should difficulties arise."

Ideally, two partners agree on what this means, happily accompanying each other to boring, but necessary, company functions and picking one another up after surgery—or not. On the often-baffling road to mutual understanding, there can be pitfalls. What one person would assume is obvious ("Of course I'll be there at the finish line of your decathlon!") to another seems optional ("I'll try to make it if work slows down"). A mismatch may shake the trust of the partners. Understanding that divergent levels of satisfying support are natural can help to allay this erosion of trust.

If you didn't feel support while growing up, you may be uncomfortable receiving it now, leaving your partner mystified that you see nothing strange with taking a cab home from the hospital. "I had planned on leaving work early to help you get home and settled," she'll say, with hurt in her voice. She would have enjoyed offering this display of love, while you cringe at being a burden. On the other hand, when someone who expects a good amount of support doesn't receive it, the hurt could feel like repudiation of love. Neglected and alone, it can be difficult to wrap your head around: *I would have done this for him. Does he not love me as much?*

HOW TO FIND A PARTNER'S SUPPORT

The keys to finding a mutually acceptable understanding are observation, communication, and respecting each other's margins. The fact that he didn't pick you up from the hospital is not likely to be a commentary on his love. But it is learned behavior resulting from his history. If you desire change, there are three steps to increase a loved one's support:

1. **Give him the benefit of the doubt.** (It is possible that he wasn't intending to be hurtful.)
2. **Don't expect him to read your mind.** (Sulking in silence will not increase mutual understanding.)
3. **Ask for what you want.** (Say it plainly: "Next time, I would appreciate a ride home from the hospital.")

If you resist receiving support, and in your view your partner is Florence Nightingale, forever hovering, repeat these three steps with the understanding that accepting support builds trust. It can be especially difficult for "male oriented people" to comfortably receive a helping hand. To avoid signs of weakness, a man's man may insist on going it alone. But, in order to become more balanced individuals, it is wise that we all access the male and female aspects within ourselves. Carl Jung, a Swiss disciple of Freud, suggests in *The Psychology of the Unconscious* that both men and women benefit by developing what he calls "anima," the inherent female expressions of their personalities. This includes opening up to emotionality, spirituality, intuitive processes, psychic sensitivities, and sharing. Once you are tuned in to this female side, accepting support feels natural.

Jung also explores the male side of our personalities—"animus"—that represents aggression, boundaries, assertion, anger, and empowerment. Balanced in both, you more easily surrender to support as well as stand firm in your own personal space. The more you become aware of your inclinations, the more you give yourself permission to accept the specific amount of support you need.

In order to discover how to effectively support one another, you must reach into the past. This Turning Point in particular hinges on early experiences. However, your history can only control you as much as you allow it to. Like the Wizard of Oz, once you see behind the curtain, the power of your past diminishes. Difficulties with protection and support are hints that it may be time to yank that curtain to the ground.

Chapter 22

FORGIVING VERSUS FORGETTING
The Boomerang Impact of Forgiveness

Sometimes it helps to be grateful for those you *don't* love. They can condescend or ignore you, and what does it matter? It doesn't hurt because you don't care. You don't love them. But that relief ends when it comes to intimate relationships. In giving your partner your love, you are vulnerable to his missteps, however innocent or cruelly intentioned. Likewise, he is exposed to your failings. Over time, it is inevitable that you will hurt one another, by virtue of your intimacy.

FORGIVE *AND* FORGET?

When wronged, you have choices: to forgive (or not) and/or to forget (or not). The common expression "forgive and forget" brings to mind a clean slate, a fresh start when you have been wronged. Certainly, forgiveness is a decision that promotes long-term happiness. By bestowing absolution, you show your partner that you have faith in him, that one mistake won't cut off your love forever. You may hope that in forgiving him, such mercy will be reciprocated when *you* inevitably offend. But those who benefit most from forgiveness are those who give it. Holding on to anger is corrosive and causes stress that can ultimately lead to a shorter life. Letting go of rage and resentment means becoming unburdened, and therefore having more room for positive emotions and growth.

As the saying goes, once you forgive, doesn't it follow that you should then forget? Not necessarily. There is a difference between holding a grudge and remembering that he publicly teased you about flunking the bar exam three times. If you forget too easily, you lose the opportunity to learn from your own and your partner's mistakes. When coupled with forgiveness, choosing to remember allows you to explore the underlying reasons for his thoughtlessness (perhaps your failure reminds him of being embarrassed by his dad's bankruptcy—and his own fear of being just like his Dad), and why his offense caused you pain (a private person, you felt his poking fun as a betrayal). Reaching such an understanding can help you see beyond the veil of your partner's motivation as well as your own.

The chart on the following page diagrams the four possible options contained in this Turning Point.

THE FORGIVING VERSUS FORGETTING QUADRANGLE

Forgiving Easily: You have the patience to study what happened and to understand the part that you played in the conflict as well as to see the humanity behind the other person's behavior. You realize that perhaps if you had been in his or her shoes you may have done the same thing.

Forgetting Easily: You have a nature that does not hold on to anger. If you also have the kind of memory that quickly forgets bad things that happen to you, then forgiving and forgetting are not particularly challenging. This choice may make your relationships easier, and potentially superficial, but not necessarily so.

Never Forgetting: If you have an excellent memory, this can be a blessing and a curse. Coupled with forgiveness, remembering when a loved one wronged you puts your feet to the fire to fight for what you believe is best, which indirectly makes demands on your partner to notice what truly bothers you. Without forgiveness, however, this choice can be defeating, causing resentment to build.

Never Forgiving: The problem with this strategy is that the hurt stays alive. Holding on to this pain will create a barrier to love's lasting pleasure. You usually never learn the part you played in the problem and you never see the authentic humanity behind whatever your loved one did.

PARTIAL IDENTIFICATION

So how do you forgive and not forget? By understanding that forgiveness is a process. It happens over a period of time as you continue to learn about yourself and also become sensitive to the underlying motivations of the one who wronged you. It can be challenging to respond with compassion toward this person. But, as you study the anger-producing event, gaining empathy affords appreciation for the shared humanity in all of us.

The key to successfully forgiving a loved one is being able to make a "partial identification" with that person. My teacher for the last two decades, Dr. Louis Ormont, who was a master group therapist and theoretician, coined that term in his book *Group Process*. It means being able to leave your own perspective temporarily in order to see the world through different eyes. Ormont calls it *partial* identification because some people are unable to establish a boundary between themselves and their partner. Once they see the world from the vantage point of their loved one, returning to their own space is difficult. The challenge is to be flexible enough to visit and then return to home base.

Many who are naturally shy find it easy to empathize with others, because they observe more than they speak. The challenge for shy people is to hold on to their version of reality. Extroverts, on the other hand, primarily see the world through their own lens, leaving them blinded to a more multilayered view of the truth. If particularly extreme in being unable to empathize, that person may have a narcissistic personality disorder. A little narcissism makes the world a more dynamic place, with lively, opinionated, and entertaining people. Extreme narcissism, in which the world must revolve around the narcissist, can cause damage to loved ones.

When you feel very angry, it is wise to question whether there is something in the event that reminds you of a part of yourself that you have difficulty facing. By employing partial identification to understand your partner's motivations, it frequently happens that you recognize a bit of yourself in their "crime." (If it greatly bothers you that she refuses to celebrate the holidays with your family, could it be that you resent the long, inconvenient trip as well, but can't admit it?) This creates a circle of empathy that furthers the process of forgiveness both for yourself and others.

USING PARTIAL IDENTIFICATION TO FORGIVE

Some of the questions to ask yourself once you open the gate of forgiveness and want to walk the path are:

- How did my particular sensitivity contribute to the disconnect?
- What part did the other person play in what happened?
- What can I do to see this event through my lover's eyes?

- Returning to my own point of view, how can this knowledge gained through empathy help me to forgive?

Imagine that your husband happily packed his golf clubs and headed down to Hilton Head on his company's dime. "No wives this time, sweetie," he said weeks ago when you expressed an interest in joining him. Months later, at the Christmas party, you overhear his colleague saying how her boyfriend fell in love with the South Carolina beaches while on the golf trip with her. Feeling betrayed and abandoned, how can you begin the journey of forgiving your husband for what now seems like a lie? Using the questions from the previous list will help you work through your pain:

- How did my particular sensitivity contribute to the disconnect? As the youngest of six children, you often felt left out growing up. You are aware that you are sensitive to feelings of abandonment.
- What part did the other person play in what happened? You believe your husband told you this trip was an employee-only affair. Why did he do that?
- What can I do to see this event through my lover's eyes? Did he want to go on this trip alone? If you discover the answer is yes, perhaps he felt his time would be best spent developing his working relationships rather than making sure you were enjoying yourself. Okay, then, why lie? Because he generally fears conflict and suspected you would perceive his choosing to go alone as abandonment.
- How can this knowledge gained through empathy help me to forgive? Armed with this bit of educated guessing, as well as knowledge about yourself, you are already well on your way to forgiveness before you've even had the initial discussion with him, in which you may discover a whole other story than what you surmised.

WHEN FORGIVENESS DOESN'T COME EASILY

Following are three common scenarios that create a difficult environment for forgiveness to take hold.

DEATH

The first occurs following the death of a loved one. In some situations, you may feel guilty being angry with the deceased for his or her departure (and you are unaware of the anger/guilt combo), so you take out your pain on those closest to you. Small missteps carry disproportionate weight, making forgiveness elusive in the storm of emotion following a loss. So if your cousin sends you a nasty e-mail after your aunt's funeral, citing the "tacky" peace lily you sent, her odd rage may be a symptom of her loss of balance in living a fundamentally different life without her mother.

SIBLING RIVALRY

Sibling rivalry is another circumstance that can hinder the ability to forgive. But what does conflict in your original family have to do with an adult partnership? Imagine that your parents favored your younger sister, showering her with love and praise while you felt overlooked, invisible. This lesson, learned young, lies beneath the surface, a raw nerve just waiting to be triggered. Thirty years later, when your husband ignores you at a dinner party, chatting up the younger, prettier hostess, your feelings of betrayal are eerily familiar. You may not even realize why forgiving him for his insensitivity is so difficult. On the surface, it wasn't that big of a deal. But keep in mind, as William Faulkner famously said, "The past is not dead. In fact, it's not even past."

INFIDELITY

The third and most common condition that makes forgiving a challenge is infidelity. There is nothing more disturbing than the person you trust the most in the world breaking his or her loyalty vow. This is because you transfer the original love that you had as an infant for your primary caretaker onto the person with whom you choose to spend your life. Then when he or she is unfaithful it shocks you to the core, reminding you of early infant insecurity, which occurs when a baby is frightened that no one is there to take care of him. As irrational as this may seem on the surface, it is completely understandable in terms of our history as creatures that take years to become self-sufficient.

ZENA AND BEN

Having met in Romania as twenty-three-year-olds, Zena and Ben moved to the United States when both were thirty-two, thrilled to be carving out a new life together. Ben found success at a cutting-edge software company in California, and they were on their way. Ten years and three children later, however, their connection was short-circuiting. Ben felt neglected by Zena's focus on the children. His hectic travel schedule exacerbated their emotional distance. Eventually, Susan, a sales manager at his company, became a shoulder to cry on—and more—when Ben was feeling lonely and abandoned. An e-mail written to Ben one day brought the affair to Zena's attention, and she reeled.

Two years later Ben was still trying to make amends. He never directly admitted he was having an affair with Susan, but acknowledged she was a very good friend while Zena was preoccupied with the kids. This made Zena see red. Zena says that had they still lived in Bucharest, where she had a large support system, she would have divorced Ben. But in the States, she felt stuck, with little life outside the children and a few friends.

Zena decided that, given her situation and the fact that Ben still had many of the qualities she had originally fallen in love with, she wanted the marriage to continue. How could she let go of her anger? Her healing process became a journey into understanding how their childhoods collided to arrive at their present moment. Zena knew she was in the role of the good girl who did everything her parents wanted and made no waves. Her mother and brother were the demanding ones; her father and she were the supportive members of the original family.

Ben's past was traumatized by a cataclysmic car crash that killed several of his family members, including his father. His resultant feelings of abandonment, coupled with an intrusive mother (also scarred by the accident), became a perfect storm of repeated emotions when he later felt neglected by Zena. Seeking comfort, he betrayed his wife. By seeing herself in her own childhood shoes as well as his, Zena was able to move past her wall of anger to the man she had married. Her empathy for herself and for her husband's lost boyhood helped her to forgive both him and herself and move forward, although she would never forget this difficult time in their lives.

Is it ever unwise to forgive? What if a loved one is abusive? Of course, there are occasions when an offense is dangerous and continuing the relationship is destructive. Then, leaving is the only option. But forgiveness is not just a tool that allows two people to continue loving one another; it is also a path to individual happiness even if your affection has died. Holding on to anger, whether or not your hurt is deep and justified, keeps the sting of the event alive. The pain is repeated over and over again in a loop that constricts your body as well as your ability to have an open heart. (There has been much research on how emotions affect the body and an abundance of literature claiming that anger can contribute to physical illness from migraines to back pain to cancer.) Forgiveness, on the other hand, is a letting go of the weight of negativity, and ultimately, a gift to yourself.

Chapter 23

GOOD SELFISH VERSUS BAD SELFISH
When Taking Care of Yourself Is Generous

This Turning Point often stumps my patients at first glance. They say, "Wait a minute. I thought being selfish is never good for a relationship." They envision selfishness as something negative—that it means being self-absorbed, arrogant, unsympathetic to others, and on and on. Of course, selfishness can be all of these things, characteristically taking the biggest piece of pie (symbolic and otherwise) always and forever, simply because it is there for the taking.

If "bad" selfish obviously resides on the negative end of the spectrum, acting absolutely unselfishly is equally damaging. Self-abdication inevitably leads to resentment. Your denied desires do not float off into the ether; they build, warping your personality so that you become your shadow-self. What's more, you do your loved ones no favors by ignoring your own needs in lieu of theirs. Few relationships thrive on such imbalance.

PUTTING YOUR MASK ON FIRST

There is another way to think about selfishness, which can best be understood by recalling the last time you flew on an airplane. Predictably, the flight attendant instructed you to put on your oxygen mask before assisting others in the event of an emergency. Why? Because without taking care of yourself first, you wouldn't be able to help those around you. Is this selfish? Well, yes. It is a perfect example of "good" selfish: By putting yourself first, you are then able to offer your stronger self to another.

Good selfish is a moving target, existing somewhere between the two extremes of bad selfish and self-denial. Knowing when it is prudent to act on your own behalf requires cultivated intuition and wise judgment. Once you are trained to listen to your own needs, you may realize your "oxygen mask" is going back to school, caring for an elderly relative, taking a vacation alone, or cultivating new friendships. The possibilities are endless, but what all these choices have in common is a desire to reach for self-expression. In doing so, you necessarily add value to your intimate relationship by developing a stronger, more dynamic you.

The idea of boundaries and barriers is especially important when exploring this Turning Point. It is easy to imagine how "bad" selfishness can build a wall between two people. If you never get up with the crying baby in the night, or you spend your money at the bar rather than on a birthday gift, don't expect your lover to reach out to you in sympathetic affection. Silence and slammed doors are more likely.

Ideally, acting on your own behalf builds boundaries that keep you steady and self-assured. If you are pleased with the path your life is on—important goals have been completed, your dreams for the future are within reach—the satisfaction you feel flows over into every part of your life. When your needs are met, you have the wherewithal to reach out to your loved ones in a spirit of empathy and generosity. Still, this choice may become complicated if your partner, despite your best intentions, perceives your efforts as bad selfish instead of good.

CONFUSING THE ISSUE

Visualize a scenario in which you and your spouse both work full-time, but in very different environments. She works alone, crunching numbers, while you are employed in a busy office with an open floor plan, where collaboration is valued. After a long week, you arrive home, thrilled to be alone or just in the company of your wife. You anticipate a weekend filled with an engrossing novel, basketball games on TV, and long solitary walks. "Don't forget we have the Anderson's barbecue on Saturday and my cousin's christening on Sunday," your wife says, shaking you out of your contentment. Having spent the week virtually alone, she is looking forward to socializing.

You have a choice: You can bow out of these activities, explaining that you value your alone time, and risk your wife's disappointment or anger. ("You only think of yourself," she may say. "How can you be so selfish?") Or, you can paint on a smile and accompany her. The latter option will surely be the one that elicits short-term harmony in your relationship. But, at what cost? Why should you subvert your desire for not being "on" (that is, not socializing) in order to join your wife? What are you losing by ignoring your own needs? These are important questions to answer because, although acting on your own behalf has the potential to cause momentary conflict, it can be valuable in the long run. By respecting your need to stay home, you not only follow your desire, but your resultant happiness may overflow, making you a better, more generous partner during the week.

MAINTAINING PERSPECTIVE

As you can see, the risk of this Turning Point is that one person may receive the partner's taking care of his or her own needs as decidedly, unpleasantly selfish. In the short term, it can be difficult to accept that a loved one's choice to follow his or her own desire at the expense of yours is not necessarily damaging to the relationship. As always, in these moments it is wise to avoid being reactive. If you were the wife in the preceding example, pausing to imagine yourself in his shoes may illuminate your husband's motivations, and lessen resentment. A smart response to his unwillingness to go out would be to suggest that the two of you reach a bargain. (If he comes to the christening, he can forgo the barbecue.) Also, choose your battles. There will be times when "no" will not work for you. Figure out when his presence is non-negotiable and when going it alone is acceptable. As well, keeping in mind the generosity he shows in other areas—like rubbing your back at the end of the day, making love to your satisfaction, and cooking most of the meals— can give you much-needed perspective.

THINK OF YOURSELF TOO

Taking good care of yourself requires thoughtful calibration. Sometimes a life direction that is truly not best for your partner requires you to put yourself first, as illustrated in the following story. When this happens in a long-term relationship, the endurance of the couple is stressed, yet the risk of forgoing something important like a job offer, or having a baby, or taking in a sick parent is also potentially detrimental. If you think back to the oxygen mask metaphor, there is no guarantee that, should you put your mask on first, you will be able to then help the person sitting next to you. Two individuals' needs may just be diametrically opposed, leaving the relationship adrift in the swirling currents of conflicting self-interest. The couple in the following story experienced just such a challenge.

ELEANOR AND GREG

Every year or so, when Eleanor and Greg were in their thirties, Greg broached the topic of children. "This window won't be open to us forever," he would say, hoping to kick-start his wife's biological clock. But each time, she cut him off, claiming her work was her "baby." And, in fact, both were enthralled with their research, so life seemed full enough.

Greg had never imagined he would end up childless. He just assumed that one day it would happen: Eleanor would suddenly feel the urge, or they would have a happy "oops!" encounter. But he never pushed her. Giving in to whatever his sweetheart wanted was his modus operandi; Greg had always had a compliant, happy-go-lucky nature, even as a child. Now seventy-three years old, Greg feels a gnawing emptiness as he watches his friends enjoy their children and grandchildren. He only hopes that Eleanor goes first, not because he doesn't love her, but rather that he cannot bear the thought of his death and Eleanor being profoundly alone: no one to mourn with her, no one to celebrate holidays, no one to call and find out how she is doing.

From Eleanor's perspective, she did exercise good selfishness. She needed the freedom to pursue her professional goals and to this day has no regrets about being childless. But Greg realizes that he should have insisted on his dream of raising a family. He was so unused to exercising the option of good selfish that he missed out on one of life's most important milestones, with no one to blame but himself for not expressing his desire. Frustrated by a life in which something is missing, Greg is compromised in offering his best self to his wife. She struggles to maintain her own satisfaction as she watches her husband sink under his malaise.

Greg and Eleanor had found that their images of the ideal family were at odds. Could they have avoided Greg's regret in their otherwise charmed life together? Pursuing individual interests within a couple dynamic begins with empathic communication. Had Greg spoken up more forcefully years ago, there surely would have been some rough waters—perhaps so turbulent that the relationship could have ended. And, had they stayed together despite the difficulties that would have been caused by their disagreement, they may still have decided to forgo raising a family. But with revealing dialogue, both would have come to better understand each other's point of view, and in time perhaps both would have opted for a change. Maybe as Eleanor came to appreciate Greg's longing, she would have engaged in more serious soul-searching about having children, rather than countering his comments with brushoffs. Possibly both would have become open to adoption, or moving to another town in order to be closer to nieces and nephews—or maybe not. Still, Eleanor and Greg would have offered themselves more intentional decision-making opportunities on the momentous life-changing subject of whether or not to have children.

STRIKING A BALANCE

Imagine a conflict such as Eleanor and Greg's as a dangerous rip-tide. As the opposing currents swirl and flow, threatening to pull your relationship under, remember: Do not fight it directly. Rather, swim parallel to the shore, waiting for an opportunity to slip from its grasp and head toward the beach. You can drown from offering too much resistance, or too little. Hold on to the faith that your emotional riptide will eventually subside, just as it does in nature. After all, in real life, no one gets it all. Allowing yourself to enjoy what you do have, without being excessively defeated by the swirl of dissatisfaction caused by what is missing, defines the art form of swimming toward a life of gratitude.

There is no guarantee of peace at home when one person's best interest is in conflict with the other's wish. But harmony at all costs may be too high a price to pay if both individuals' needs are being thwarted. Sometimes out of conflict a creative moment is born.

The person who has exercised good selfish is now able to bring something new to a long-term love—a fresh perspective on work, family, or how to stay happy.

Looking back over the short history of the United States, we can clearly see American society's struggle with this idea of selfishness as right or wrong. Pursuing self-interest was what the country was originally founded on—a philosophy that is even written into our Constitution. But, as time went on, society vacillated. The 1950s saw women as vessels of self-sacrifice, with little outlet for their own desires outside of the home. Then, with the rise of the baby-boom generation, the pendulum swung sharply, ushering in an era of self-centered "me-ness." The repercussions of this are vast—a quagmire of economic shortsightedness and a planet in peril. Can people now find a "pursuit of happiness" not at the expense of others? We can begin by practicing good selfishness and striving for balance in our love relationships.

Chapter 24

FAMILY LOYALTY VERSUS SELF-INTEREST
The Downside of Attachment

Two people falling in love over a romantic meal may think they are alone. Lost in a world of their own, they gaze into one another's eyes, unaware that crowding around the table are his overbearing mother (and her difficult mother before her), her silent dad and depressed mother, and—most important—their younger selves. As you mature and develop adult relationships, the past affects the present. While some of us acknowledge how our histories have fortified us for the here and now, for others the stubborn tug of unfinished childhood challenges creates obstacles in moving forward.

Ideally, your caregivers sent you off into the world with a solid sense of being well grounded. This feeling of security gave the future—even if uncertain—a glow of possibility. Waving goodbye, you pursued your dreams without being pulled back by the drag of incompleteness. In this scenario, you chose your life according to your own self-interest.

But breaking free of the past, for some, can be difficult. Over-attachment to your original families may interfere with taking a chance on adult love, or cause you to damage relationships once you are in them. While in some sense the word *loyalty* is the foundation for devotion to your relatives, lovers, and country, in this chapter the implied reference is to a dependent connection to your family of origin that interferes with charging full steam ahead.

PAM AND GINA

Pam and Gina are not only excellent daughters, they are also the bedrock of their sprawling Italian family, organizing reunions, hosting baby showers, and attending to the sick. Whether the event is happy or sad, these twins take charge. Professionally successful, attractive, and fit well into their forties, all the Donatellos agree: Pam and Gina's parents are lucky to have such winning daughters.

But the sisters share one trait that has in some ways ruined their lives. Can you guess what it is? Well, if their respective goals were to circle around other people's lives, then they have succeeded. But if they had hoped to establish homes for themselves—filled with their own partners and children—they have thus far failed. Both women have had lovers, usually someone else's partner or unavailable boy/girl toys. But neither has carved out a lasting, intimate adult relationship. Comfortable in the bosom of their family, both have sat on the sidelines, letting an opportunity to live with their own peers, perhaps having a child or two or more, flow by. Sadly, neither Pam nor Gina planned for her life to turn out this way.

ATTACHMENT THEORY

Is there a reason these sisters dip their toes into the deep end of life, rather than diving right in? The fear of taking the plunge is rooted in early childhood. Again, we turn to attachment theory pioneer John Bowlby, who suggested that the quality of nonverbal communication between a mother and her child determines an infant's secure or insecure feelings about herself. Taking this one step further, the frame of reference that the infant develops determines how free she is in adulthood to think, feel, remember, and act from her own vantage point. The more reliable the original attachment, the more comfortable she is in letting go of family and forging her own life.

People who describe a sound connection in infancy feel more open to finding strangers outside of the family circle to fall in love with and even marry. They are able to perceive these partners as a steady source of support and love. Securely attached to the original love object, they transfer this desire for closeness to their partners during times of threat and uncertainty. More comfortable than others in the face of criticism, tension, and insensitivity, they put a positive spin on the struggles of intimate life and are only half as likely to get divorced as their less-secure peers.

If, on the other hand, an infant develops an anxious attachment to an original love object, he or she feels as an adult that others do not give enough and are not reliable sources of intimacy and love. Such people have greater dissatisfaction, cynicism, distrust, and criticism. These tendencies formed from the earliest mother/child bond infuse every moment of their intimate relations. The insecurely attached infant grows to be an adult whose ability to think flexibly is constrained—and thinking in a fixed pattern makes maintaining a home with an outsider difficult to accomplish.

THE ROLE OF PARENTS

From the attachment theory research, it would seem that Pam and Gina developed an apprehensive bond with their primary love object—their mother—and this has influenced their choices thus far. Here are two people who have selected family loyalty over self-interest; lasting love for their immediate relatives, but not for themselves. For these sisters, the problem originated with a mother who was anxious and controlling and a father who let mom run the household unchallenged. A minor sniffle sent everyone to the emergency room; in lieu of hugs, the house was sanitized in a never-ending battle against germs. The girls took these precautions to heart: The world is a scary place. Their loyalty to each other also made separation problematic. The twins were foxhole buddies in a childhood fraught with "disease" and danger. They agreed: Best to stick with what you know.

Insecure attachment can also develop if the primary caregiver—usually the mother—is absent, either physically or emotionally. It may also be the case that if the father is absent, the child questions the reliability of an adult partner to be present through thick and thin. In either scenario, the baby or young child is incessantly reaching for the absent parent, wordlessly conveying, "Love me, I need you, be with me, merge with me." If his efforts are frustrated, the distress becomes embedded, a lasting lesson that life is unsatisfying. The ache of this early failure echoes well into adulthood, making him averse to the risk of emotional turmoil. The possibility of a second heartbreak becomes untenable. Early trauma makes later traumas feel twice as intense. It may even be the case that this now adult is still preoccupied with winning Mommy's (or Daddy's) love. Loyal to a fault, proving himself to his parent through professional successes and by sticking close to home, he has limited space for another, more mature love.

Even beyond infancy, parents have the power to stymie their kids' courage to embrace their own definitions of living a good life. Think of today's notion of the "helicopter" parent. In general terms, the mom or dad who hovers over a youngster—hoping to keep him safe, performing at peak levels, without a moment of unscheduled time—risks saddling the child with doubt about his ability to stand on his own two feet. The unease this parent conveys is instilled in the offspring, who may develop a wary view of the world.

As well, the current trend of young adults moving back in with mom and dad—or never leaving—hampers risk-taking. When parents have difficulty pushing their children out of the nest, it may evolve for some into an impediment to finding a life partner. Beyond the practical considerations (who wants to bring a date back to their childhood bedroom?), the fantasy becomes, How will anyone ever be as devoted to me as Mom and Dad? Why should I risk finding—and losing—a love when what I've got right here is unconditional?

GENDER VARIATIONS

The pull of family loyalty over self-interest is an addictive, gravitational force that is difficult to break. You end up the moon to your parents' sun—both a blessing and a curse. Choosing self-interest could mean marrying someone who doesn't fit in with the family, or moving out of state, or not taking over the family business. How ungrateful! How disloyal! These moves risk disapproval from the original font, where all power seems to lie. It's easy to see why sticking with family is tempting.

Interestingly, this Turning Point differs along gender lines. For women (although, exceptionally, not for Pam and Gina), attachment to the original family tends to be more fluid. Accustomed to forming bonds with others—and biologically rewarded by a flood of feel-good oxytocin, a neuropeptide that promotes devotion and is released during nonverbal displays of love—some women find it easier to remain attached yet independent. In most cases, you can come home, new babies in tow, man trailing behind with the bags, and be embraced by mom and dad. There is a sense of happy expansion, and—ideally—belonging.

A man, however, goes out into the world often unknowingly plagued by a vague sense of disloyalty when he meets someone and settles down. Up to this point, mother was his primary female love object, a force so potent he feels he has no recourse but to choose *between* her and his new lover. This black-and-white tendency becomes problematic as his loyalty to both the old love and the new is stretched and torn, with no comfortable middle ground on which to stand. On the one hand, some men are overly devoted to mom, unable to make a reasonable break. They tend to resist geographical separation, and can frustrate wives and lovers by unfair comparisons to mom's fabulous cooking and historically unwavering affection.

On the other side of the spectrum are men who succeed in shutting out mom in a misguided attempt to escape her apron strings. This cutoff takes self-interest to an extreme, resulting in an underlying sadness and anger that permeates family life. Difficult to pinpoint, this sense of dissatisfaction can cause marital tension. Tempers may flare when the subject of family visits comes up. "We haven't seen your parents in almost a year," she'll say. "Why don't we go down and show them the new baby?"

"And open ourselves up to their criticism?" he may say grumpily, exaggerating the potential for an unsatisfactory visit. Or he may brush off the idea, claiming too much work or some other excuse. That he spends the weekend sulking is no surprise. His sadness has real potency, as it is at once self-inflicted and also stems from the powerful emotions of early childhood.

EMBRACING SELF-INTEREST

Living according to your own self-interest means embracing your adulthood comfortably, with a flexible approach to the new. Sure, there will be disappointments, but a life fully lived means taking risks and learning from them along the way. Doing what is right for you—even if it means making a mistake—is empowering.

How can people who suffer from problematic early childhood attachments learn to choose self-interest over family loyalty? Is it possible that the bond with your original family can become less restricting, allowing you the self-determination to go forth and conquer? Clinical psychologist David J. Wallin is a strong proponent of extricating oneself from an embedded point of view by finding new "reference points." In *Attachment in Psychotherapy,* Wallin maintains: "Relationships of . . . insecure attachment and/or unresolved trauma lead to rigid, and sometimes brittle, attentional strategies that restrict our ability to update old internal models on the basis of new information and to consider experience from multiple perspectives." In plain language, insecure parent/infant attachment makes us resist looking at multiple perspectives of the same reality. This is a problem if one hopes to have an empathic connection with another person, especially a loved one.

Being trapped in family loyalty often goes hand-in-hand with isolation between the self and self (for example, my family expects me to become a doctor and I can't disappoint them even though I wish to be a professional musician), as well as between the self and others. Seeking out new forms of community can sometimes break the spell and become a catalyst for change. Joining a therapy group, religious organization, book club, or gym can expose you to other people's thoughts. In such circumstances, some bit of sacred knowledge you've held on to since childhood may be debunked. Hearing your bridge partner casually mention how she moved continents to be with her lover may help you re-evaluate your family's mantra: *We stick together no matter what!* When a new friend laughs at how she chased her husband until he finally had dinner with her, she may have no idea of the effect this anecdote has on you. But your mother always said calling a boy was shameful! You wonder how many opportunities you missed by living according to this stale advice rather than following your own inclinations.

With training, you can leave your embedded points of view so that other people's experiences become emotionally relevant. You can guide yourself to open up to new beliefs, feelings, and perspectives. As you move away from tired and worn thinking, family loyalty takes a more flexible position and you may notice new possibilities for evolving self-interest on the horizon waiting to leap into your life. This embrace of personal power is strengthening. When you return to your family of origin relaxed in your own worldview and ready to share it, you will be surprised to find that your newfound security encourages those around you to join in the pursuit of an expanded life for all.

Chapter 25

JOY VERSUS HAPPINESS
Embracing What Lasts

Several years ago, my husband and I were vacationing at a ski village in Utah when a blizzard blew in from over the mountains. The hotel enforced a mandatory lockdown, thus dashing my desire to hit the slopes. Disappointed—I am passionate about skiing—I bemoaned the "lost" day as the winds howled outside. Then, a funny thing happened: I began to surrender to the cozy warmth of our room. A feeling of deep contentment crept in as I sank down into solitude without feeling an obligation to go out and have fun. This unforeseen circumstance taught me a lesson: Enjoying the outdoors gives me happiness, but staying inside, thinking, writing, dreaming, meditating, is where I found joy on that particular day.

Interestingly, the seed for this book was planted that very afternoon as I contemplated why so many of us confuse the core concepts that are the foundation of giving and keeping love. My solitary reflection gave birth to the first several of the eventual twenty-five Turning Points that are the heart of this book, and it is no accident that I've elected to end with Happiness versus Joy. For if you consistently choose the boundary-building Turning Point in each pairing, joy necessarily follows. It is the natural outcome of thoughtful, intentional behavior.

BEYOND HAPPINESS

The distinction between happiness and joy can be elusive because joy has a tendency to hide in plain sight. Whereas happiness is worldly—it feels great to buy a new possession or go on an exhilarating run—joy is at once basic and more profound. It means transcending temporary pleasure-seeking and instead offering up a part of yourself to a loved one, to an idea, or to gratitude for being alive. Joy lasts, while a delightful meal or a trip you enjoyed soon becomes a memory, fading with time. This is not to imply that happiness is something to avoid—only that it is self-driven and narrow, and therefore over time risks distracting you from love's ideal: appreciation for the extraordinary gift of sharing your life with another.

Between the sixth and the fifth century B.C.E. in China, Confucius offered his thoughts about finding joy in the world around us. He believed that accessing our own kindness, seeing our collective humanity, and respecting others are joyful, satisfying experiences. The Chinese word for this is *jen*, or bringing the goodness in others to completion. I have witnessed its emergence as a surprising outcome of the recent financial collapse here in New York.

With job losses skyrocketing and economic recovery on an uncertain horizon, many people are being forced to re-evaluate what makes life worth living. No one is happy to have lost half their savings, or that vacations this year will be modest or nonexistent. But people do seem more content about buying fewer things, cooking their own meals, and staying home with loved ones. More time to spend with their children, and more time in bed with their partners, is part of the collateral "damage" of our current crisis. And, according to many of my patients, this reprieve from the rat race is a reminder of the joy—the *jen*—of shared time, space, and even struggle.

DACHER KELTNER AND THE BIOLOGY OF JOY

Joy is based on biological foundations that have had a lasting effect on our evolution as a species. In *Born to Be Good,* Professor Dacher Keltner of the University of California, Berkeley, describes emotion research that was based on the correlation between facial expressions, brain measurements, and Far Eastern philosophy. Covering evolutionary biology from animals to early man to us, Keltner begins and ends with the basic definition of joy: How cooperation, social intelligence, and empathy are the secret to both the survival of our species and to joy.

Science has new measurements to examine microscopic facial muscle movements that signal devotion, touch that indicates appreciation, and playful vocal tones that transform conflict. We can now also isolate brain substances called neurotransmitters as well as regions of the nervous system that promote trust, caring, devotion, forgiveness, and play. All of these findings point to the evolutionary nature of human kindness and cooperation and indicate that our survival actually maintained itself through cooperative behavior rather than, as Charles Darwin's thesis is usually misunderstood, a competitive phenomenon in which the physically strongest wins. This is commonly referred to as survival of the fittest.

The bottom line is that humans are hard-wired for joy. When we give to others, reward centers of the brain hum with activity. Generosity produces a chemical high, a fact that will come as no surprise to anyone who has ever volunteered in a soup kitchen or otherwise helped someone in need.

Professor Keltner's findings dovetail with the emphasis of this book, which is that joy comes from building sensitive boundaries between yourself and the one you love and tearing down the walls that lead to isolation. It is through these boundaries that compassion—the root of joy—freely flows. He emphasizes that perpetual conflict runs through human social life, but a rich array of capacities defuse it, such as appeasement, forgiveness, play, teasing, and laughter. These are all behaviors that, even in our most difficult encounters with a loved one, tear down barriers and allow love to bravely shine forth.

People are designed to care about things other than the gratification of desire and the maximizing of self-interest—the basic drives that support the pursuit of happiness. The emotions that promote a meaningful life are, rather, organized according to an interest in the welfare of self and others. In an intimate relationship, when you love in a spirit of generosity, it feels joyful because you are predisposed to empathy and kindness. Despite life's inevitable challenges, childhood trauma, and your less attractive personality traits, this capacity for joy resides within you. The twenty-five Turning Points you have discovered in this book are the key to accessing it.

HENRY AND NORA

Nora had always imagined that she and Henry would spend their twenty-fifth wedding anniversary celebrating with friends or on a cruise somewhere sipping mai tais. As they drove silently upstate to the jail, she closed her eyes and imagined she was somewhere—anywhere—else. Today was the first day of freedom that their oldest son, Greg, had seen in eighteen months. *Twice as long as I carried him*, Nora thought sadly, remembering those days of happy anticipation. His conviction for armed robbery had shocked the family to the core. But, Greg had always pushed the limits; his finally getting caught was almost a relief.

They waited for nearly an hour before they heard a metallic clang, followed by the sight of Greg's skinny frame emerging from the building. At twenty-four, still sullen like a teenager, he slid into the backseat with a mumbled "Hey," and kept his dark sunglasses on. Nora and Henry had agreed to use the five-hour drive to calmly talk to Greg about his future. But one look at his disrespectful son was all it took for Henry to unleash a year and a half of pent-up rage. Nora tried in vain to be the voice of reason as the two men screamed accusations and threats. When they finally dropped Greg off at his sister's house, he slammed the door hard enough to make their ears ring.

Where was the joy in all of this? Arriving home wrung out, Nora couldn't even take comfort in the fact that they had acted as a team—Henry was alone on his warpath. But later that night, after they had made love, they both cried for the lost little boy they had raised. It wasn't the anniversary they had wished for, but in a way it felt more authentic than a big party. Between them stood decades of love and failure and laughter and sad days like the one they had just lived through. Nora's heart ached for Henry, while Henry hated being unable to save her from this awful situation. Within their mutual grief was a deep joy for their unwavering connection and shared experiences. The waning hours of their anniversary were spent crying and laughing.

Henry and Nora's circumstance illustrates how joy can be accessed even when happiness eludes us. Thomas Schelling, a Nobel Prize–winning economist, suggests in *The Strategy of Conflict* that emotions are involuntary commitment devices that bind people to each other in long-term mutually beneficial relationships. Your autonomic nervous system enables you to adapt to ever-changing conditions. Once your varying emotions are in sync with your shifting conditions, you can find joy by becoming aware of the opportunities to snatch gratitude when you can, despite the outside world's difficulties. Therefore, happiness may be responsive to what is happening around you, but joy can be maintained from within. Given life's unpredictability, this is certainly a powerful theory: No matter the storms that rage, the ability to access joy is always and forever at your fingertips.

THE JOY OF TOGETHERNESS

In long-term relationships, joy deepens with time. When you fall in love, it is certainly mind-blowing. Your happiness soars as hearts pound; the sexual chemistry is off the charts. These heady early days begin a journey that can take you down several paths—some positive and some painful. You have seen from the Turning Points in this book that there are many barrier-building behaviors that can send you skidding away from lasting love. However, if you learn to avoid these missteps, over time you move past the initial phase of happiness with a loved one and into deeper waters. Like Henry and Nora, if you can weather the storms of life together with an undercurrent of compassion and generosity, the reward is a joyful partnership.

Psychology professor John Gottman, in his popular book *Why Marriages Succeed or Fail*, claims he can predict with 92 percent accuracy which of the hundreds of couples he interviewed will eventually divorce, and which will stay together. When partners show high levels of contempt, criticism, defensiveness, and withdrawal, their long-term prospects are dim. On the other hand, couples that demonstrate respect, kindness, and humor are better able to deal with conflict and tend to have lasting partnerships. These findings go hand-in-hand with Professor Keltner's research on human cooperation, as well as the themes found in this book.

Your capacity for joy is like an untapped well—you only need the tools to access it. Gottman's couples with a propensity for togetherness understand that the keys to a joyful, lasting love are found in empathic connection. This bond relies on your very humanity and—according to Keltner—your humanity relies on this very bond. As simple as this palindrome-like idea is, the difficulties of daily life can make steady cooperation and loving kindness for your partner challenging. But remember, the twenty-five Turning Points break down the everyday decisions that can make a real difference between joy and despair. If you are consistently inclined to choose the positive, boundary-building behavior within each Turning Point, your chances for finding and keeping a lasting love are high.

If happiness is the hand reaching out to take what it desires, joy is the hand that caresses, consoles, and gives. Joy is an expansive feeling that includes awe for the miracle of your own life as well as the world around you. It transcends your own self-serving interests in favor of a larger whole. When Buddha attained enlightenment, he realized that suffering is rooted in self-centeredness and desire—feelings that encourage you to pursue happiness. If you can shed the illusion that these desires will lead to sustained joy, then, according to Buddha, goodness will arise from within.

The goal of lasting love is to root yourself within a stimulating relationship so that both partners can flourish and expand to realize increasing possibilities. Loving kindness, compassion, right talk and action, as well as humor and affection, all support a joyful union. With patience, one Turning Point at a time, you can move closer to this dream. And if the dream proves to be elusive, look for the silver lining. There is always more to learn, more to grow toward, more to appreciate, more to experience. I am honored to have accompanied you on this voyage, and wish you joy on your journey to lasting love.

APPENDIX
The Emotional Turning Point Test

The Emotional Turning Point Test is a cutting-edge tool of social science that I developed in cooperation with Dr. Emily Jacobs and Rachel Potek. We constructed this test while both were my PhD students in the applied psychology department at New York University, where I am an adjunct professor. It uncovers the extent to which barriers instead of boundaries are created. The more you are able to construct boundaries between yourself and others, the more you benefit from relationships and flourish in your own individuality.

Following you will find the twenty-five Turning Points, placed inside of vignettes, with four possible responses to each story. Each answer awards 0 to 2 points. The most responsive answer receives a score of 2. The least responsive indicates reactivity, and awards 0 points. The remaining two choices show a degree of establishing personal boundaries, resulting in a score of 1 point for either one. (Following the questions is an answer key that indicates which answers award 0, 1, or 2 points.) Within the overall score, profile analysis reveals strengths and weakness in three areas: communication, personal power, and flexibility.

When completed, this test will indicate where your personal boundaries are well-established and where you may be creating barriers to a satisfying love relationship. You will then possess identified opportunities for improvement. Remember: The higher your score, the better your boundaries; the lower your score, the more barriers you are erecting.

Read the following vignettes and select the resolution that most reflects your tendencies.

PART I: FLEXIBILITY

1. **Responsive versus Reactive**
    Your partner's business is going bankrupt. You:

    a. become depressed and edgy, without saying why.

    b. say you are scared, then listen to how he/she feels about it.

    c. provide a forum for discussing the stress, and express confidence you both will survive.

    d. don't let it affect your mood, and privately chalk it up to a learning experience.

2. **Good Judgment versus Critical Judgment**
    You don't believe in dating someone who is married. Bo, who is attractive and has been separated for a year, asks you out. You:

    a. yell at him, "how dare you, you are still married."

    b. agree to go, saying to yourself, "Who cares? He is attractive."

    c. agree, saying that normally you only date single people but you're willing to go since the separation is a year old.

    d. ask him to call in six months, knowing you could miss an opportunity with a special person.

3. **Expressing Your True Self versus Conforming to a Role**
    You wish to have nightly family dinners and set the table with heirloom silver and china the way you were raised. Your spouse wants to go to the gym before coming home and this is too late for the children to eat. You:

    a. make one special day a week for family dining.

    b. store the heirloom stuff in the closet, and try to get everyone together even if it's just for pizza.

    c. create a dining environment, daily, for you and the children despite the absence of your spouse.

    d. let everyone eat what, where, and when they want.

4. **Autonomy versus Isolation**

    Sally is 40 years old and wants to get married. You are 38 and feel that Sally is perfect, if only she was 10 years younger. You:

    a. marry her but keep your bachelor apartment and finances separate until you are more comfortable with the union.

    b. realize that her age is not the problem; you are resisting for other reasons that may be due to fear of taking such a big risk.

    c. marry her.

    d. break up.

5. **Surrender versus Submission**

    Your partner's father visits from London and they stay up every night talking and watching sports on TV. You:

    a. hear the TV all night and say nothing, thinking to yourself that he only visits every once in a while.

    b. tell your partner that Dad has to stay at a hotel from now on.

    c. come to an agreement about quiet after a certain hour and use earplugs if you want sleep before the agreed-upon hour.

    d. become exhausted and irritable, especially to your partner's dad.

6. **Establishing Space versus Neglect**

    You love telling jokes and holding an audience. When your quieter partner joins you and your colleagues for a work dinner, you:

    a. hold court by being hilariously funny and entertaining.

    b. remain quiet, except to address your significant other.

    c. tell a few jokes, and ask questions of your partner.

    d. stay quiet.

7. **Patience versus Passivity**
   You have been seeing your partner for two years and are anticipating movement toward marriage. As the months go by with no indication of this, you:

   a. keep hoping to yourself and begin resenting your partner.

   b. during a close moment ask your partner how she/he feels about commitment in general and—more specifically—to you.

   c. think to yourself that you'll bring it up in six months, as your partner is presently distracted by work worries.

   d. tell yourself that if there's no sign of a future here within six months, you will give your partner an ultimatum.

8. **Benign Boundaries versus Emotional Tyranny**
   Alex refuses to come back to therapy because he can't handle Lena's anger. In Lena's shoes, which of the following responses would you choose?

   a. Ask him to move out, as you cannot go on without his agreeing to come to therapy.

   b. Hide your anger; forget about therapy.

   c. Continue to express your anger despite his refusal to come to therapy.

   d. Seek help from your therapist as to how to build a bridge to Alex.

9. **Awareness of Limits versus Emotional Recklessness**
   Your partner wants to adopt a baby. You love your partner, but are still unsure about staying together long-term. You:

   a. fill out adoption papers together, despite your doubts.

   b. agree, but secretly start planning your exit.

   c. after a discussion where you admit being unsure, agree to adopt a child.

   d. break up to demonstrate that there is too much pressure.

10. **Embracing Change versus Preserving the Status Quo**
You want to leave Wall Street, where you work on the trading floor. You're worried about your finances, given how comfortably your job has allowed you and your partner to live. You:

   a. don't want to bring it up now, because you just refinanced your mortgage.

   b. leave trading for a small investment firm.

   c. become a history teacher.

   d. stay, and when you have a hard time sleeping, resent your partner.

PART II: COMMUNICATION

11. **Taking Responsibility versus Blame**
You take an unscheduled trip to Mexico and don't call while away. Reacting to your partner's angry inquiries, you:

   a. counter by saying, "But you ignore me too."

   b. say, "You ignore me when I am home. Still, it was wrong to not call you. I am sorry to cause you stress."

   c. apologize and say, "It was insensitive of me. I need to work on putting myself in your shoes."

   d. say, "I was in a third-world country. By the way, what are we having for dinner?"

12. Needs versus Wants

You are a building contractor and volunteer firefighter who knew many people who died on 9/11. You ask your partner, a freelance writer, to move with you to New York while you help rebuild near Ground Zero. Your partner wishes to stay in Connecticut near elderly parents. You:

a. agree and think perhaps you were too needy.

b. say, "I need the support because I am sad and uptight. The work is a daily reminder of my losses."

c. say, "I want company. Who am I going to have dinner with?"

d. say, "I need the support, but you decide what is best for you."

13. Detach versus Withdraw

You are nervous about your brother going to a war zone. Hearing you express this, your partner shouts, "Get over it!" You:

a. don't speak to your partner for a week.

b. observe his reaction and say, "We have to talk about the shouting."

c. keep going, feeling sad and alone inside but behaving normally.

d. become upset and demand an apology.

14. Speaking Up versus Silence

Your partner travels for work most weeks. Feeling abandoned, you become attracted to your 23-year-old golf caddy. You:

a. alert your partner that you are starting to become attracted to the caddy.

b. keep your frustration to yourself but ask to play golf with your partner instead of the caddy.

c. tell your partner you are feeling left out, and ask whether you could you brainstorm ways for more togetherness.

d. have an affair with the caddy.

15. Giving the Benefit of the Doubt versus Making Assumptions

Your partner comes home late smelling of alcohol. You:

a. ask him/her to sleep in the living room, believing whatever happened was bad for the relationship.

b. are angry and worried, yet wait until morning to find out what happened.

c. give a hug, fall fast asleep, and check it out in the morning.

d. think nothing of it; what's a little fun now and then?

16. Intimate Listening versus Hearing

Your partner wants to spend Thanksgiving with friends; you have a desire to spend it with your extended family. You:

a. say, "Thanksgiving is non-negotiable."

b. acknowledge that your family can be overwhelming, saying, "I hear you, but we can't go to friends this Thanksgiving. Maybe next year."

c. continue reading the paper while your partner talks about how his friends feel like family to him. You get the essence of what your partner is trying to tell you about loneliness and feeling overwhelmed by strangers.

d. hear your partner wants time with others, agree that your family can be overwhelming, and say, "How about inviting our friends for Christmas Eve?

17. Influence versus Control

You rediscover religion. You:

a. insist your family attend services with you.

b. leave religiously influenced thoughts of the day on the refrigerator door.

c. go to services, inviting whoever wants to come.

d. go to services yourself and keep your experience private.

18. Constructive Criticism versus Destructive Criticism

Your partner, who is dyslexic, is considering studying Chinese. You:

a. volunteer that it is very hard.

b. say "I know you can do it" without being asked.

c. ask if your partner would want to brainstorm this idea with you.

d. say to yourself that this is none of your business.

PART III: PERSONAL POWER

19. Deciding versus Craving

You want to lose 20 pounds for an upcoming wedding. You are invited to a buffet party at a four-star restaurant. You:

a. eat whatever you see.

b. eat a piece of the cheesecake and salad.

c. eat broccoli and salmon.

d. decline the invitation.

20. Fighting Fair versus Fighting Unfair

You are unhappy. Your partner tells you: "Then leave. But you get no money, and the children stay with me." You have these choices in mind:

a. go to couples therapy, where you discover your partner's hurt over rejection and reveal your frustration over being misunderstood and threatened.

b. get the children on your side and find a lawyer to take the divorce case on consignment who assures you about your entitlement to a fair share of the money.

c. freeze your partner out and refuse to have sex.

d. keep your frustrations private and have sex to soften the tension.

21. Support versus Protection

Your loved one stutters with strangers. You:

a. finish your partner's sentences when the stuttering begins.

b. offer time for your partner to get it out.

c. make a plan about what kind of help would be appreciated.

d. walk away during stuttering moments.

22. Forgiving versus Forgetting

Your partner ignores you the first time you go to visit his family. When you get home, you:

a. scream and storm out of the house.

b. notice it and are disappointed, but choose to let it go.

c. forgive your partner and stop yourself from feeling bad as you know it was a stressful weekend.

d. explain how invisible you felt, and discuss how to avoid a repeat of this situation.

23. Good Selfish versus Bad Selfish

You have back pain and your doctor recommends daily yoga (which you love) to strengthen your spine. You:

a. take the advice and show understanding to your partner during complaints of so much time away from home.

b. allow your partner's complaints to influence your decision, and don't take the doctor's advice.

c. tell your partner that his objections won't stop you from going to yoga daily.

d. resent both your doctor for putting an unrealistic demand on you and your partner for complaining; use your free time to read books.

24. Family Loyalty versus Self-Interest

Your partner asks you to give up a job you enjoy in order to start a business with him. You:

a. give up your job and devote yourself to working with him.

b. cut your hours back to help develop the business.

c. quit your job, but spend most of your time on eBay when you are in the office.

d. refuse to consider the request.

25. Joy versus Happiness

You and your partner are planning a special trip. You:

a. take little interest in it.

b. look forward to rekindling love.

c. are interested in an adventure, less in whom you are with.

d. agree to visit with your partner's brother instead of going to Hawaii.

ANSWERS

1. Responsive versus Reactive
    a.—0
    b.—2
    c.—1
    d.—1

2. Good Judgment versus Critical Judgment
    a.—0
    b.—1
    c.—2
    d.—1

3. Expressing Your True Self versus Conforming to a Role
    a.—2
    b.—1
    c.—1
    d.—0

4. Autonomy versus Isolation
    a.—1
    b.—2
    c.—1
    d.—0

5. Surrender versus Submission
    a.—1
    b.—1
    c.—2
    d.—0

6. Establishing Space versus Neglect
    a.—1
    b.—1
    c—2
    d.—0

7. Patience versus Passivity
    a.—0
    b.—2
    c.—1
    d.—1

8. Benign Boundaries versus Emotional Tyranny
    a.—1
    b.—0
    c.—1
    d.—2

9. Awareness of Limits versus Emotional Recklessness
    a.—1
    b.—0
    c.—2
    d.—1

10. Embracing Change versus Preserving the Status Quo
    a.—1
    b—2
    c.—1
    d.—0

11. Taking Personal Responsibility versus Blame
    a.—1
    b.—2
    c.—1
    d.—0

12. Needs versus Wants
    a.—0
    b.—2
    c.—1
    d.—1

13. Detach versus Withdraw
    a.—1
    b.—2
    c.—0
    d.—1

14. Speaking Up versus Silence
    a.—1
    b.—1
    c.—2
    d.—0

15. Giving the Benefit of the Doubt versus Making
    Assumptions
    a.—1
    b.—1
    c.—2
    d.—0

16. Intimate Listening versus Hearing
    a.—0
    b.—1
    c.—1
    d.—2

17. Influence versus Control
    a.—1
    b.—1
    c.—2
    d.—0

18. Constructive Criticism versus Destructive Criticism
    a.—1
    b.—1
    c.—2
    d.—0

19. Deciding versus Craving
    a.—1
    b.—2
    c.—1
    d.—0

20. Fighting Fair versus Fighting Unfair
    a.—2
    b.—1
    c.—0
    d.—1

21. Support versus Protection
    a.—1
    b.—1
    c.—2
    d.—0

22. Forgiving versus Forgetting
    a.—0
    b.—1
    c.—1
    d.—2

23. Good Selfish versus Bad Selfish
    a.—2
    b.—1
    c.—1
    d.—0

24. Family Loyalty versus Self-Interest
    a.—1
    b.—2
    c.—0
    d.—1

25. Joy versus Happiness
    a.—0
    b.—2
    c.—1
    d.—1

This test gives a fair indication of your personal trends in the areas of flexibility, communication, and personal power. The higher the score, the stronger your boundaries; the lower the score, the more barriers you have erected. Barriers interfere with satisfying lasting love. If your score is below 10 in any or all of these categories, refer to the corresponding chapter(s) to discover where you may be encountering confusion or difficulties. Then, once you have absorbed the lessons of each Turning Point, take the test again and watch your score improve!

REFERENCES

Atkinson, Brent J. *Emotional Intelligence in Couples Therapy.* New York: W. W. Norton & Company, 2005.

Baruch, Rhoda, Edith Grotberg, and Suzanne Stutman. *Creative Anger: Putting That Powerful Emotion to Good Use.* Santa Barbara, CA: Praeger Publishers, 2007.

Bergman, Martin S. *The Anatomy of Loving.* New York: Ballantine Books, 1987.

Bowlby, John. *Separation: Anxiety and Anger, Attachment and Loss.* London: Hogarth Press Publications, 1973.

Cagen, Sasha. *Quirkyalone.* San Francisco: HarperCollins, 2004.

Coontz, Stephanie. *Marriage, a History.* New York: Viking Press, 2005.

Dumm, Thomas. *Loneliness as a Way of Life.* Cambridge, MA: Harvard University Press, 2009.

Fisher, Helen. *Why We Love.* New York: Henry Holt and Company, 2004.

Freud, Sigmund. *Remembering, Repeating, and Working-Through.* In J. Strachey, Ed. & Trans., *The Standard Edition of the Complete Psychological Works of Sigmund Freud* (Vol. 12, pp. 147–156). London: Hogarth Press and the Institute of Psychoanalysis, 1958. (Original work published 1914.)

Gardner, Howard. *Frames of Mind: The Theory of Multiple Intelligences.* 10th Anniversary Edition. New York: BasicBooks, 1993.

Gilbert, Daniel. *Stumbling on Happiness.* New York: Alfred A. Knopf, 2006.

Goleman, Daniel. *Emotional Intelligence.* New York: Bantam Books, 1995.

Goleman, Daniel. *Working with Emotional Intelligence.* New York: Bantam Books, 2006.

Gottman, John. *Why Marriages Succeed or Fail.* New York: Simon & Schuster, 1995.

Gottman, John M., and Nan Silver. *The Seven Principles for Making Marriage Work.* New York: Crown Publishers, 1999.

Jacobson, Bonnie. *Love Triangles.* New York: Crown Publishers, 1991.

Jacobson, Bonnie. *If Only You Would Listen.* New York: St. Martin's Press, 1995.

Jacobson, Bonnie. *The Shy Single.* New York: Rodale Press, 2004.

Jacobson, Bonnie. *Intimate Listening.* (Republished Bloomington, Indiana: iUniverse, 2009.)

Jung, Carl. *The Psychology of the Unconscious.* Tel Aviv: Dvir Co., Lt., 1973. (Original work published 1917.)

Keltner, Dacher. *Born to Be Good.* New York: W. W. Norton, 2009.

Kipnis, Laura. *Against Love.* New York: Pantheon Books, 2003.

Leigh Brown, Patricia. "Even if You Can't Buy It, Happiness Is Big Business," *New York Times*, 27 November 2008. National News section.

Lewis, Thomas, Fari Amini, and Richard Lannon. *A General Theory of Love*. New York: Vintage Books, 2000.

Phillips, Adam. *Side Effects*. New York: HarperCollins, 2006.

Maimonides, Moses, translated by Friedländer, Michael. *The Guide for the Perplexed*. New York: Forgotten Books, 1925.

Margalit, Avishai. *The Ethics of Memory*. Cambridge, MA: Harvard University Press, 2002.

Markman, Howard J., Scott M. Stanley, and Susan L. Blumberg. *Fighting for Your Marriage*. San Francisco: Jossey-Bass, 2001.

Maslin, Bonnie. *Picking Your Battles: Winning Strategies for Raising Well-Behaved Kids*. New York: Hyperion, 2007.

Maslow, Abraham. *Toward a Psychology of Being*. 3rd Edition. New York: John Wiley & Sons, Inc., 1998.

McMahon, Darrin M. *Happiness: A History*. New York: Atlantic Monthly Press, 2006.

Ormont, Louis. *The Group Therapy Experience*. New York: St. Martin's Press, 1992.

Sartre, Jean-Paul. *Existential Psychoanalysis*. Chicago: Henry Regnery Company, 1962.

Sartre, Jean-Paul. *The Transcendence of the Ego.* New York: Farrar, Straus and Giroux. (Original work published 1937.)

Schelling, Thomas. *The Strategy of Conflict.* Cambridge, MA: Harvard University Press, 1963.

Schwartz, Barry. *The Paradox of Choice.* New York, HarperCollins, 2004.

Siegel, Daniel. *The Mindful Brain: Reflection and Attunement in the Cultivation of Well-being.* New York: W. W. Norton, 2007.

Squire, Susan. *I Don't: A Contrarian History of Marriage.* New York: Bloomsbury, 2008.

Thompson, Robert Farris. *Tango: the Art History of Love.* New York: Vintage Books, 2006.

Wallin, David J. *Attachment in Psychotherapy.* New York: Guilford Press, 2007.

Wallerstein, Judith. *The Unexpected Legacy of Divorce.* New York: Hyperion, 2001.

INDEX